IN THE SHADOW OF EMPERORS

THE CULT IN ROMAN CYPRUS

IN THE SHADOW OF EMPERORS
THE CULT IN ROMAN CYPRUS

Agnieszka Ochał-Czarnowicz

Kraków 2018

Publication financed by the National Science Centre, Poland (grant no. DEC-2012/07/N/HS3/00858)

Reviewer
Dr. Piotr Kołodziejczyk

Proofreading
Steven Jones

Author of the photographs
Agnieszka Ochał-Czarnowicz

Cover design and typesetting
Elżbieta Fidler-Źrałka

Photo on the cover
Petra tou Ramnou—the mythical birthplace of Aphrodite (by Agnieszka Ochał-Czarnowicz)

© Copyright by the Alter Publishing House and Agnieszka Ochał-Czarnowicz
First Edition, Kraków 2018

ISBN: 978-83-64449-72-7 (Alter Radosław Palonka)
ISBN: 978-83-956708-0-0 (Jagiellonian University, Institute of Archaeology)

Wydawnictwo Alter Radosław Palonka
ul. Śliczna 30B/43
31-444 Kraków
phone: +48 606-781-823, e-mail: alter@wyd-alter.pl
http://www.wydawnictwoalter.pl

Printed in Poland:
MAZOWIECKIE CENTRUM POLIGRAFII
ul. Mikołaja Ciurlionisa 4
05-270 Marki

Contents

Preface 7

Introduction. Cyprus during the Roman period: Some remarks 9

Sacred landscape 13

Religion 27

Towards monotheism 55

Conclusions 57

References 63

Appendix 77

Plates 79

PREFACE

As Jody Michael Gordon underlines in his PhD thesis *Between Alexandria and Rome: A Postcolonial Archaeology of Cultural Identity in Hellenistic and Roman Cyprus* (2012), the history of Cyprus has long been viewed as a linear succession of imperial powers. From this viewpoint, cultural change under imperial rule was understood as a natural process of the conquered passively accepting the empire's superior culture. When imperial culture was in some respect not fully accepted by the local community, this was often interpreted as an act of resistance. In recent years, however, methodical and epistemological development in classical archaeology has called into question the existing interpretations of cultural changes during the Hellenistic and the Roman period. New perspectives in humanities discourse, the postcolonial theory in particular, have caused scholars to re-evaluate traditional assumptions. The emphasis falls on the complexity of cross-cultural interaction between the colonizing and colonized groups. Epistemological changes have also occurred in Cypriot archaeology. Detailed GIS analysis of old archaeological data as well as new excavation works including those in Amathous, Idalion, Nea Paphos and in the rural sites such as Athienou-Malloura, Panayia Ematousa have led to new interpretations of how Cypriot culture changed under Roman rule. Instead of a one-way Romanization process, both local Cypriot and foreign archaeologist have begun to perceive the impact of the Roman culture as a developing, pluralistic dialogue of different trends reflecting the island's multicultural past. *The cult of heroes in Roman Cyprus* project financed by the Polish National Science Center awarded on the basis of decision number DEC-2012/07 /N /HS3 /00858 has made a small contribution to the broader vivid academic discourse on Roman Cyprus. The research focused on the religious landscape in general and the worship of heroes in particular. The worship of heroes is one of the most fascinating aspects of the Greek religion. Heroes were the essence of the society from which they came. According to G. Heedren (1991), the main difference between the worship of heroes and Olympic gods lies in the geographical limits of the cult. While a hero-cult was most often restricted to a particular locality, the worship of the Olympian gods was usually widespread. Hence, tracing the heroes' cult gives a good insight into the local religious tradition, which is very important within the discourse about the complexity of the Romanization process. In the culture of any society, there are values which form the basis of its identity and nothing reflects them better than the religious sphere.

INTRODUCTION
CYPRUS DURING THE ROMAN PERIOD:
SOME REMARKS

Annexation

Cyprus, the third largest island in the Mediterranean, came under Roman domination in 58 BC. The story is told in Plutarch's biography of Younger Cato (Plutarch, Cato Minor: 34-38) who was dispatched to implement the annexation. Forced to abdicate, King Ptolemy committed suicide; his possessions and treasure were auctioned off and the land was annexed under the rule of Rome (Bekker-Nielsen 2004, 55). Both the surviving literary and epigraphical evidence from that first phase of the Roman administration indicates that Cyprus was under the responsibility of the proconsul of Cilicia, although little is known about that period (Hill 1940, 226-7, 254-6; Mitford 1980, 1291-2). Numismatic evidence confirms literary accounts (Appian, Bellum Civile: 5.1.9, 5.6.52; Cassius Dio: 42.35.4-6) of the restoration of Ptolemaic rule at least for some period of time between 48/7 to 30 BC. Julius Caesar, as Roman consul, returned the island to Egypt and it effectively fell under Egypt's control. The mint of Paphos resumed its activity in 47 BC and bronze coins were struck with the names of Cleopatra and Ptolemy XV Caesarion[1]. Furthermore, Mark Antony confirmed the donation of the island to the Ptolemies (cf. Plutarch, Anthony: 54.4; Cassius Dio: 49.41.1-3). Our knowledge about the Ptolemaic restoration and their government of Cyprus is more than just fragmentary and the local reaction to it remains frustratingly obscure (Hussein 2014, 79). Finally, after the defeat of Anthony and Cleopatra VII, Octavian regained control of the island in 30 BC. The status of the island and how it was administered from 30-27 BC is unknown. From 27 BC, Cyprus was governed through legates endowed with imperium pro praetorie.

Administration

In 22 BC, Cyprus was returned to senatorial rule and became a public province governed by proconsuls. To prevent a proconsul from gaining too much power, the administrative change was to shorten to the length of the year (Michaelides 1990, 115). Potter (2000, 786)

---

[1] Bicknell (1977) proposed an alternative sequence according to which Cleopatra ruled the island between 44-41 and regained it around 35

has observed that men who governed public provinces often did not rise above the praetorship. This means that Cypriots not obtained much out of a good relationship with the proconsul and had limited access to high ranking Roman nobility. Very little is known about most of the Roman proconsuls of Cyprus themselves. The Cypriot proconsul, along with his retinue of civil officials and his cohorts praetoria, was the source of all imperial authority. He oversaw various aspects of provincial administration (e.g. resolving disputes, overseeing the maintenance of roads, ensuring that cities did not bankrupt themselves, maintaining public order and morality) and served as the key contact between the Cypriots and the emperor. Because of the island's position in an area of the Roman Empire that was stabilised by pax romana, the proconsul was not in charge of an army that was permanently stationed on the Island (for discussion on exceptions see: Potter 2000, 813; Hussein 2014, footnote 251). Several other officials assisted the proconsul in the administration of Roman Cyprus. The legatus could be assigned to some of the proconsul's less important judicial functions whereas the quaestor played the key role in terms of monitoring provincial finances and collecting taxes. Beside the above-mentioned officials, imperial procurators—officials of equestrian rank who administered the emperor's property or imperial monopolies—were also stationed on the island. The best example of this office in Cyprus was the procurator of the copper mines.

Internal division

The internal (if any) division of the island is not clear. The 2nd century AD geographer Claudius Ptolemy in his Geographia (5.14.1-7) divided Cyprus into four districts: western with Nea and Palai Paphos, sothern with Kourion, Amathous and Kition, eastern with Salamis and the north one spreading from Karpasia till Arsinoe. There is no doubt that Salamis and Nea Paphos were considered as the primate cities of east and west Cyprus respectively but a picture of the status of the particular places is far from complete (cf. Mitford 1980, 1308-1341). Unfortunately, no epigraphic evidence of a complete list of cities of Roman Cyprus exists. The poleis of Roman Cyprus are recorded by several ancient authors (e.g. Strabo, Geographica: 14.6.1-3; Pliny Elder, Historia Naturalis: 5.130) The literary sources vary and do not provide us with a complete picture of the civic status of Cypriote cities. The most generally accepted list of the poleis is the one presented in the seventh century AD by Georgius Cyprius (Descriptio Orbis Romani: 1096-1110) including Kition, Amathous, Kourion, Paphos, Arsinoe, Soloi, Lapethus, Keryneia, Tamassus, Chytroi, Karpasia, and Salamis (*Figure 1*). The Roman authorities permitted the Cypriot cities some degree of local political autonomy. Many civic offices established under the Ptolemies continued to function. Most cities had an oligarchic boule selected by archons. It was responsible for municipal affairs such as: civic roads, management of public property, building projects, grain and water supply, the collection of local taxes etc., and the awarding of honours to various Roman and local worthies. In accordance with the 'Roman' way of creating public space, both administrative and local decisions brought to the poleis the large-scale public buildings constructed under Augustus, Antonines, and the Severian dynasty in particular. The urban space became

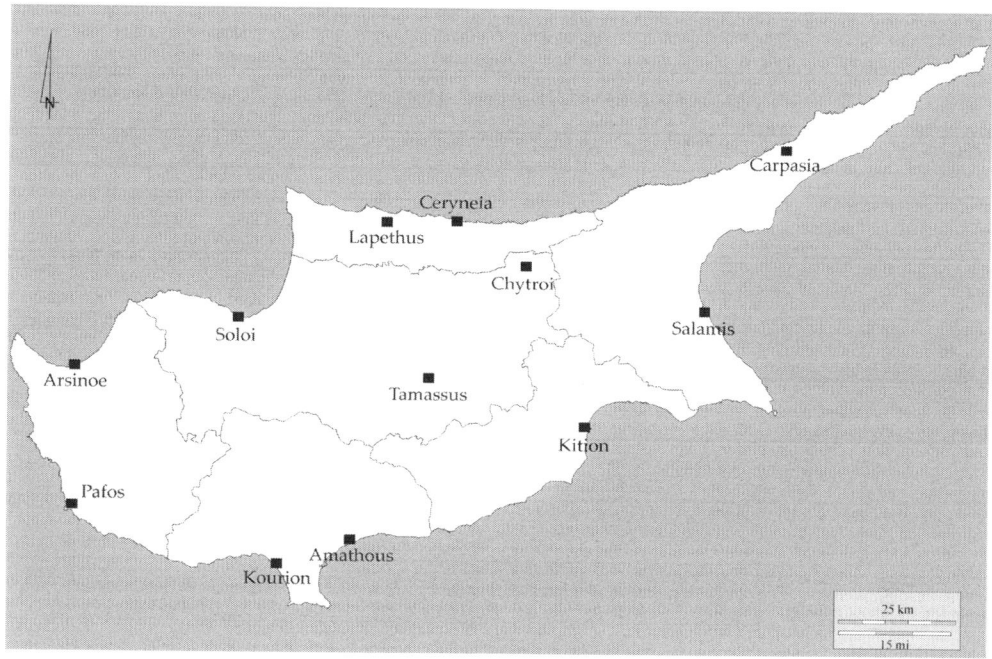

Figure 1. Map of Roman cities.

very important in the culture sphere. From epigraphic evidence we know that local elites underlined their social status by adopting different 'municipal' functions such as the gymnasiarch, ephebarch, or agonothetes. Those, who wanted to express their status beyond the municipal level, participated in the Koinon Kyprion. This institution, characteristic of the Roman era, is also mentioned in two inscriptions dated to the late Hellenistic period (Mitford 1961a, 37, 39; Papantoniou 2012, 154). All Cypriote cities participated in the koinon. Organized around the imperial cult, the koinon was an institution responsible for the organisation of various religious festivals, had the right to mint copper coins, and was capable of representing Cyprus' interests corporately (Michaelides 1990, 120). Some of its high priests became ambassadors to the emperors and travelled to Rome.

Archaeological data reveals that the government of Cyprus was rather efficient, with mostly positive interactions with locals and local communities, although the name of one of proconsuls—Theodorus—was cursed in a defixio tablet found at Amathous (Wilbrun 2005, 210; Hussein 2014, 67-69).

Economy

Roman organisation of the island's economy was founded upon pre-existing Hellenistic structures. Although metallurgy and shipbuilding remained the principal element of the so-called 'heavy industry' of ancient Cyprus (Raptou 1996, 256), still their value should not be overestimated. The mines yielded profit for the island but their significance declined with time, and as early as in the beginning of the 4th century AD, the copper industry had almost faded into insignificance. The importance of ship building (cf. Ammianus Marcellinus: 14.8.14) may have lasted slightly longer. Archaeological enquiry also demonstrated that production of mineral medicaments (Michaelides 1996, 139), fine pottery, and coarse wares (Hayes 1967, 65-74; 1977, 96) were at least equally important elements of the economic sphere. Continued profit for the Cypriote economy was also provided by trade in agriculture products. Literary sources (e.g. Strabo, Geographica: 14.6.5) indicate that Cypriote agriculture relied mainly on the cultivation of such basic products as grain, grapes for wine, and olives for oil. Marine resources played a minor economic role. Fish are rarely mentioned in sources and there is no evidence for the production of salt fish nor garum on a large scale (Bekker-Nielsen 2004, 60). Unfortunately, not much is known about the organization of Cypriote agriculture during the Roman period. Bekker-Nielsen (2004, 61) has estimated that around the beginning of our era the ratio of urban to rural population was not more than 1 to 5. Although a gradual movement of people to major city-centres is noted, the change in settlement patterns was not so great and, after an intermediate period, the late Roman Cypriote countryside flourished (cf. Rautman 2000; Manning et al. 2002). There were no major latyfundia nor imperial estates on the island. The economy, as Michaelides (1996, 140) suggested, lay in the hands of wealthy landowners and those involved in commerce. At the beginning of Imperial rule, the cities of Cyprus were connected by good Romans roads. They played an important role in the process of accelerating trade development. It is worth mentioning that trading activities around the Cypriot coast also increased from the Hellenistic period (Moore 2003). The importance of the island in maritime networks is underlined by the large number of ports, harbours, and anchorages. These are identified both by archaeological investigation and are listed in ancient literary sources (Leonard 1995, 227-242). Used as enterports, points for intra-regional trade, or just as stops for ships traveling to other destinations, they demonstrate the complex range of maritime trade activities (Moore 2003, 229). Thanks to them, Cypriots were enriched through their participation in the imperial economy with markets that consumed goods from distant regions (Potter 2000, 842-49).

The island of Cyprus and its people functioned as a proconsular province governed by the Roman senate until Diocletian transferred its administration to the praetorian prefect of Antioch in 293 AD. Hence, for over 320 years, Cyprus' political, economic, and cultural life was conditioned by its geopolitical position as a distant imperial province administered from Rome.

SACRED LANDSCAPE

Change in the sacred landscape?

The detail development of Cypriote sanctuaries in the Roman period has not yet been the subject of in-depth research. While many Cypriote sites date from the general Greco (Hellenistic)-Roman period, based on data collected during the project (see also Appendix), and research conducted by Ulbricht (2008) and Papantoniou (2012), it can be said that only about 36 sanctuary sites (including urban, extra urban, and rural ones) provide reliable evidence of religious cult during the Roman times (*Figure 2*). This number should be confronted with the catalogue of 106 sanctuary sites from the Hellenistic period (Papantoniou 2012, 382-384) and with more than 80 Early Christian basilicas (Papageorghiou 1985) which similarly to the ancient sanctuaries played an important role both in religious life and in the process of inscribing social memory (Papantoniou, Vionis 2017). Such a disproportion to the Hellenistic sanctuaries first observed by Papantoniou (2012, 157) could be interpreted either as a fundamental change in practice or as a sudden decrease in religious activities. In the case of Roman Cyprus, both theories were proposed. However, a closer look at the religious landscape reveals a rather more complicated picture.

Gradual development

On the religious map of Roman Cyprus, most active sanctuaries, like during the Ptolemy reign, were located along the cost, mainly in the major cities. They included the sanctuary of Aphrodite at Palaipaphos in the southwestern part of the island, the temple of Aphrodite at Amathous and Apollo Hylates at Kourium on the southern coast, and the temple of Zeus Olympios at Salamis in the east (*Figure 3*). All these sites preserve evidence of religious practice dating back to the early Iron Age while they were given a more monumental form under the rule of the Ptolemaic dynasty when the island began to be ruled as one organism. There was no break in the functioning of any Cypriote sanctuary that may be connected with Roman annexation of the island nor any sudden change in religious practice. From the Annales of Tacitus (3.62), we know that Cypriote asked to retain the rights of asylia for three main sanctuaries: Palaipaphos, Amathous and Salamis. The relevant passus is as follows:

> *The Cypriotes followed with an appeal for three shrines — the oldest erected by their founder Aërias to the Paphian Venus; the second by his son Amathus to the Amathusian Venus; and a third by Teucer, exiled by the anger of his father Telamon, to Jove of Salamis.*

Figure 2. Map of Roman sanctuary sites.
1 Achna, 2 Amargetti, 3 Amathous-acropolis, 4 Amathous Agora, 5 Amathous Agora, 6 Amathous North Gate, 7 Arsos, 8 Chantria, 9 Chytroi, 10 Golgoi-Hagios Photios, 11 Idalion-Moutti tou Arvili, 12 Idalion-City Sanctuary, 13 Keryneia-Regatikon, 14 Kition, 15 Kourion-Apollo Hylates, 16 Larnaca-Salines, 17 Ledra, 18 Lefkoniko, 19 Louroudjina, 20 Malloura, 21 Nea Paphos-Phanari, 22 Nea Paphos-Garrison's camp, 23 Nea Paphos-Fabrica, 24 Nea Paphos-Septimus Sever, 25 Palaipaphos, 26 Phasoula, 27 Pyla, 28 Pyroi-Elia, 29 Rantidi, 30 Rizokarpasso (Chelones), 31 Salamis, 32 Soloi-acropolis, 33 Soloi-Cholades, 34 Tamassos, 35 Tamassos, 36 Voni

An inscription found in reused material in Amathousian agora indicates that this prestigious right was indeed confirmed (Hermary 2015, 36).

Traditional patterns

Wright (1992, 188), who wrote a compendium of Ancient Cypriote architecture, underlines that some of the Cypriote religious tradition was a *sanctuary as a prime unit in itself situated in natural surroundings and more or less independent of any urban development.*

Such a description suites the Roman sanctuary of Aphrodite in Palaipaphos perfectly, which played the most significant role, as Gordon (2012) clearly demonstrated, in the process of building and transferring Cypriot identity. The first monumental shrine on the site was erected in c. 1200 BC. Although, we cannot now reconstruct it in every detail, it is certain that it represented the so-called Near Eastern type of court sanctuary with a large open cult area and a smaller, covered holy-of-holies *(Figure 4)*. When the last

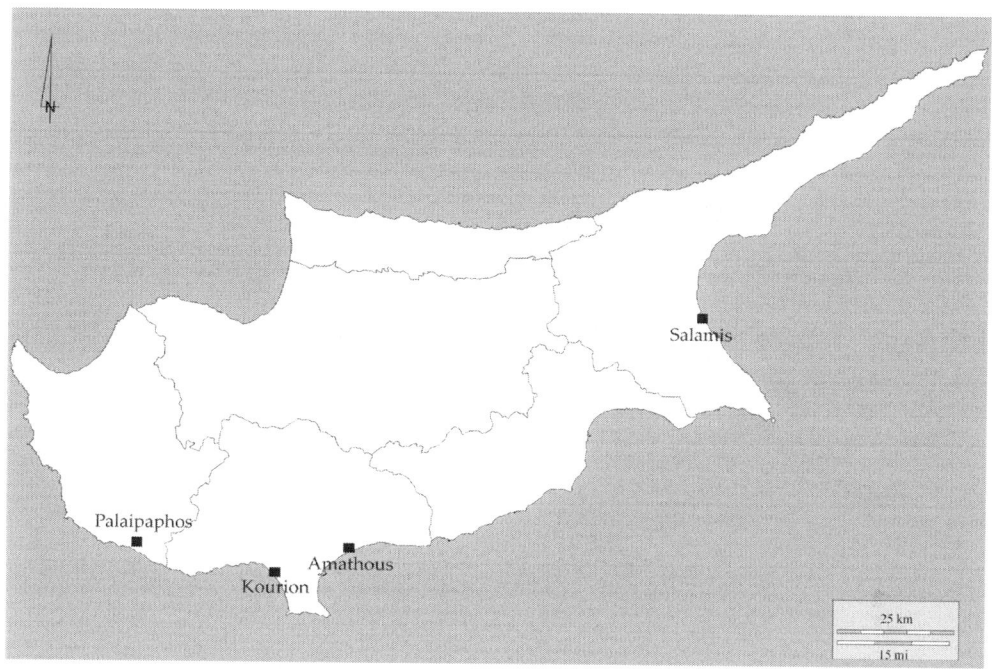

Figure 3. Map of main Roman sanctuary sites.

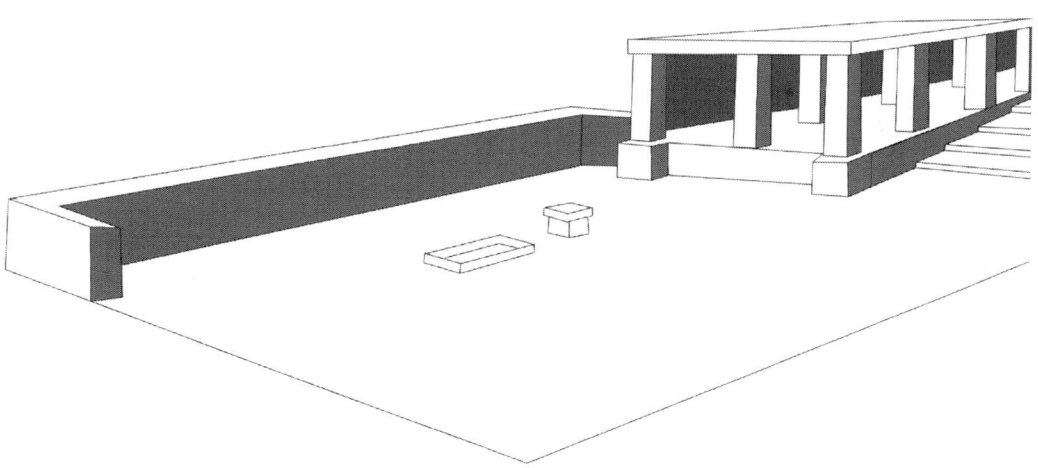

Figure 4. Sanctuary in Paphos—reconstruction of early phase. Drawing based on Maier 2010, 44.

King of Palaipaphos, Nikokles, moved his capital at the end of the 4th century BC to the newly-founded Nea Paphos, the sanctuary retained its importance. Gradually, it became the first pan Cypriote, and later an important pan-Mediterranean pilgrimage centre.

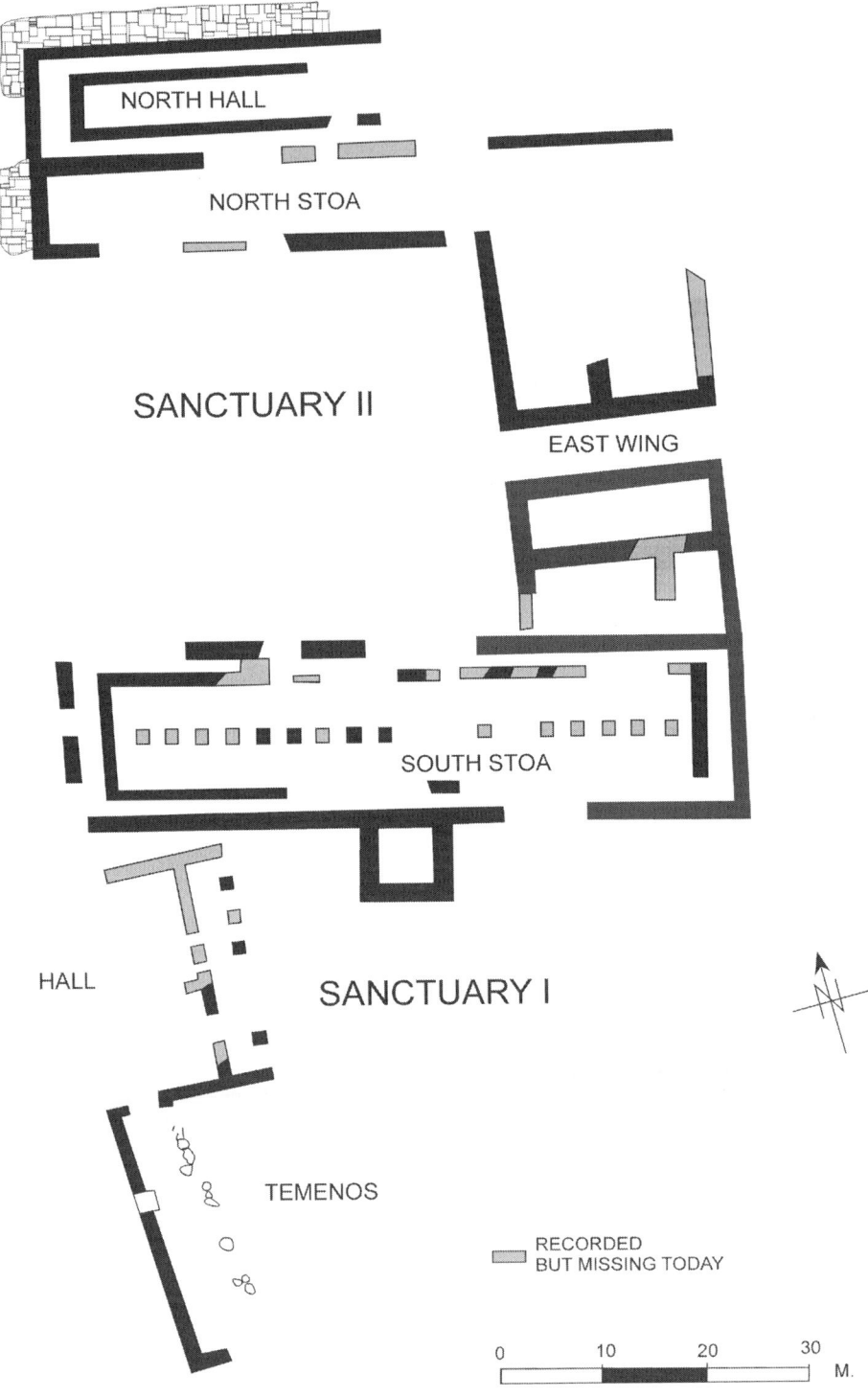

Figure 5. Sanctuary in Palaipaphos—plan. Drawing based on Maier 2010, 40.

Unfortunately, the archaeological remains of Roman town and sanctuary have not been examined in detail. After the damage of 77/78 AD earthquake, the whole structure had to be rebuilt (*Figure 5, Plate 1*). In the new part—the so-called Sanctuary II—emphasis was focused on structures which seem to have served as a cultural banqueting hall for pilgrims visiting the sacred place (Karageorghis 2005, 33). The architecture of the heart of the sanctuary remained close to the traditional Cypriot temenos and the cult statue of the goddess kept the aniconic shape of baetyl (Wright 1992, 188). The image of the tripartite Palaipaphos sanctuary on the Roman coins issued by the Koinon Kyprion from the 1st–3rd centuries (Amandry 2016; *Figure 6*) underlines the significance of archaic religious elements up to at least the middle Roman period.

Figure 6. A representation of the temple of Aphrodite at Palaipaphos on coin from the reign of Caracalla—drawing based on the Encyclopedia Biblica.

The extra mural sanctuary site at Soloi-Cholades constitutes another example of a traditional Cypriote sanctuary. It was excavated and published by A. Westhlom (1936) from the Swedish Cyprus Expedition. Based on his stratigraphy, it seems that in the Roman period five temples functioned: B, C, D, E, and F. Originally, the sanctuary was dedicated to the worship of Aphrodite. In the first, Hellenistic phase of the sanctuary, steps and a small vestibule provided entry to a longitudinal court behind which laid to a traverse court with a squarish building—a temple (*Figure 7*). Adjacent to the inner court were the remains of a structure which may have been a priest's house. In the subsequent building phase, the original cella remained unchanged but the outer courtyard was enlarged and in the place of the possible priest's house, a second building (Temple C) was constructed. In this way, Temple A was replaced by a double temple (*Figure 8*) whose existence is most probably noted by Strabo (Geographica: 14.6.3). It seems that the so-called Temple D was contemporary to the above-mentioned structures. From the East, stairs led up to an open courtyard. At the rear of the court, a narrow terrace was built in front of a two-cella building. Although the sanctuary of Soloi-Cholades was developed late in the Ptolemaic and early Roman period, its architecture followed the model of an oriental sanctuary consisting of large square courts connected to small rooms which formed the holy-of-holies. The same plan, with minor modifications, was also used later, when temple E and F were built. As time passed, the buildings increased in number, became more monumental and more connected with each other, although still none of Cholades structures acquired the form of a Greek-style temple (Papantoniu 2009, 285).

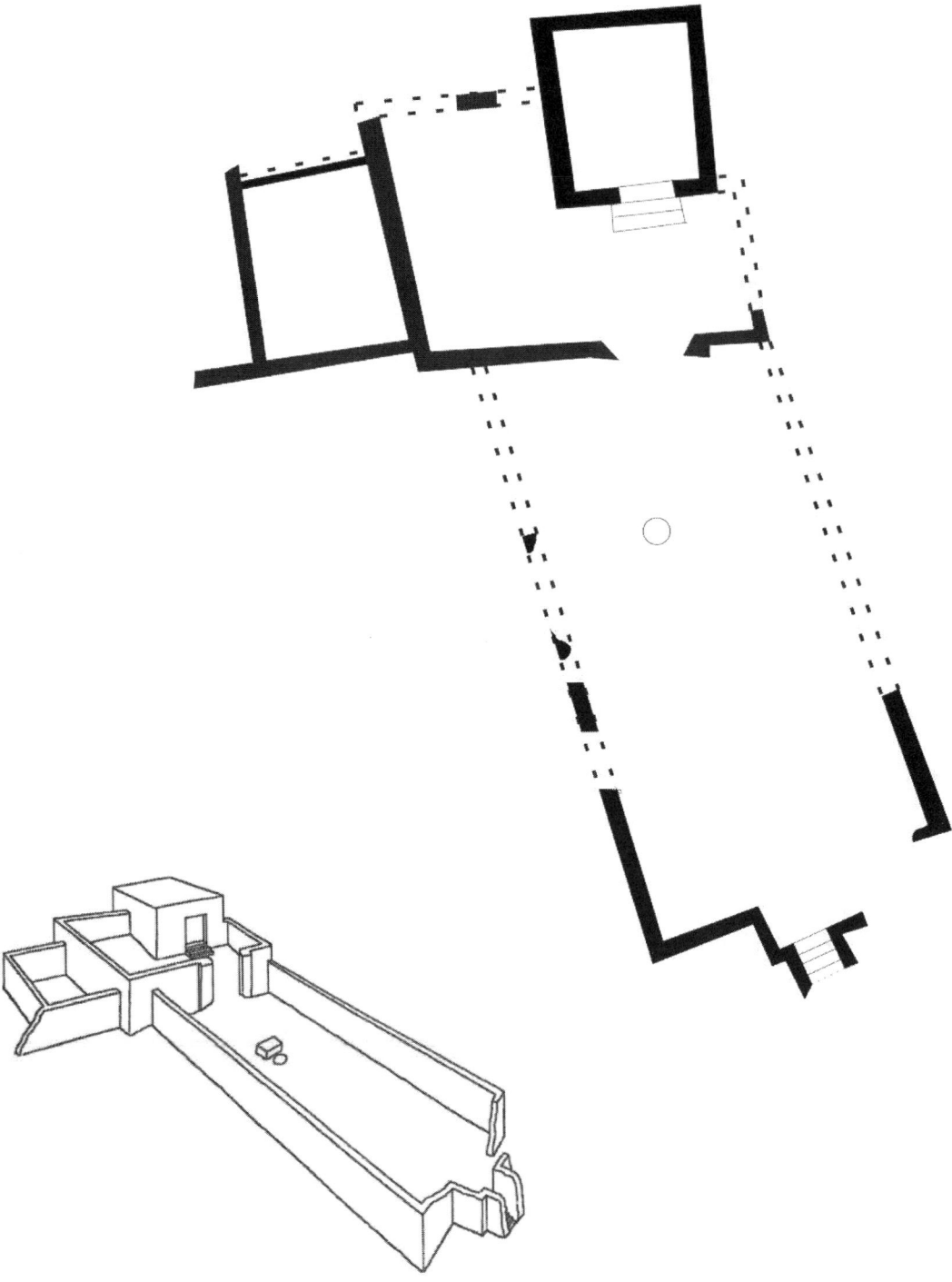

Figure 7. Temple A in Soloi-Cholades plan and reconstruction—drawing based on Westhlom 1936, 90.

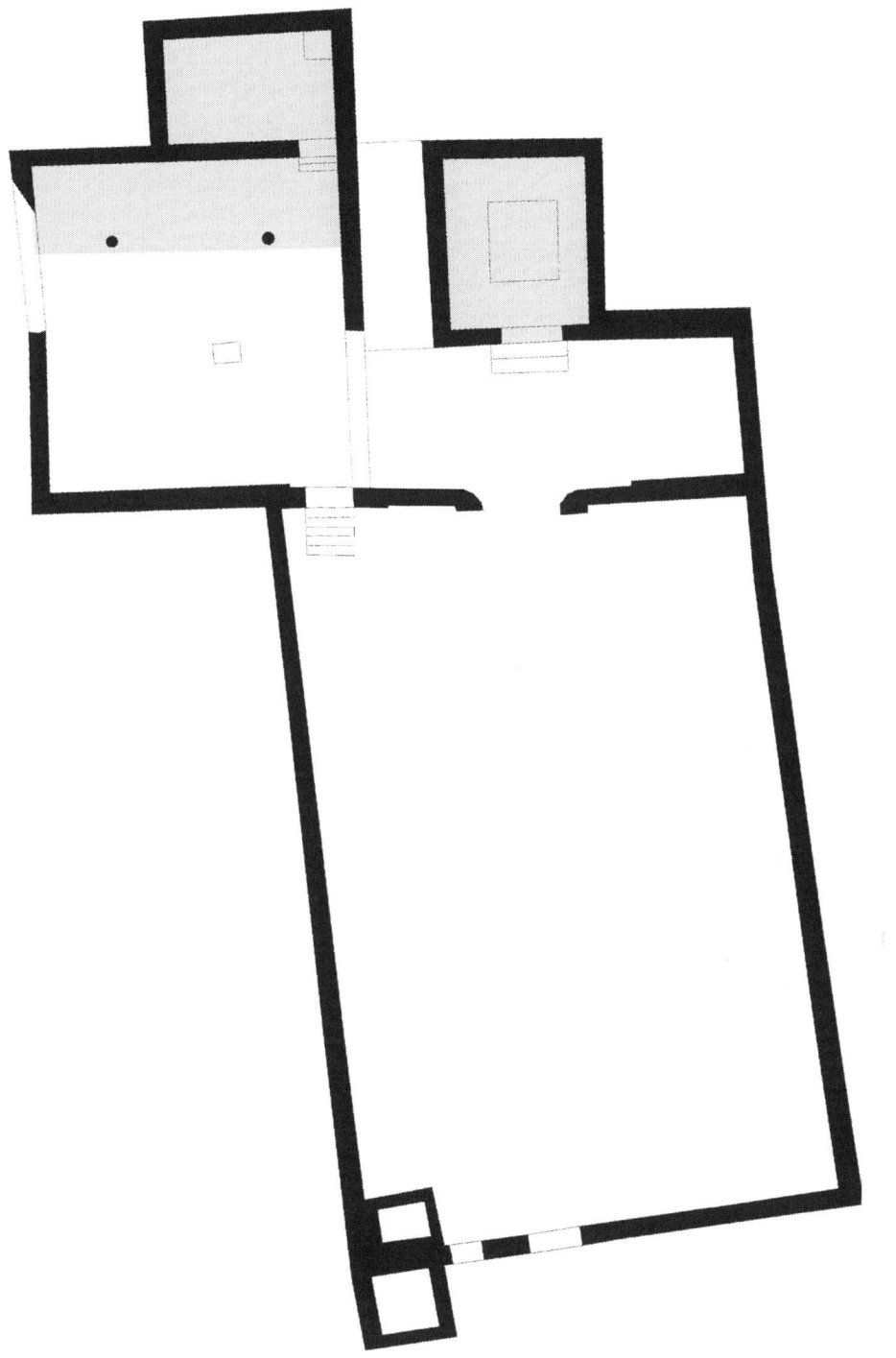

Figure 8. A double temple (Temple B and C) in Soloi-Cholades plan and reconstruction —drawing based on Westhlom 1936, 90.

Greek temple and the change in architecture

Contrary to the traditional architecture of Palaiphos and Soloi-Chloades, the classical Greek model was introduced to other costal sanctuaries during the late Hellenistic period. Unfortunately, none of the Hellenistic structures were left un-rebuilt and their remains cannot provide any major evidence of the first Greek temples in Cyprus. During the Roman period, the Greek temple model of a sanctuary was fully developed. Its architecture was based on East Mediterranean trends with a major Syrian influence, including backs of blocks left rough. In each case, the 'Greek' temple was one of several religious structures. Because of its long history, there was no one single model for sanctuary arrangement.

Although the importance of the Salaminian sanctuary was so significant in Roman times that the cult statue of Zeus, which stood in the temple, was chosen to be used on a coin reverse, not much is known about its architecture. It seems that the Hellenistic Greek temple was rebuilt twice—first during the early Roman period and then, as the inscription suggests (Mitford 1971, 198), during the Hadrian reign. The Roman sanctuary had a large court with a multi-arched gateway. The temple built on a high stylobate had a square cella at the rear. Fallen column-drums and Corinthian capitals of a considerable size suggest an impressive building (cf. Argoud et al. 1975, 124-136; *Figure 9*).

Figure 9. Salamis—temple of Zeus. Photo by the author.

Much more data is available on the temple of Aphrodite in Amathous Acropolis. Its main Roman construction phase (cf. Aupert and Hermary 1981, 1030) is dated to the last quarter of the 1st century AD—after the earthquakes of 77/78. Although, the edifice was completely destroyed during the erection of an early Christian basilica, the systematic excavation works carried out by a French mission yielded enough architectural elements to propose reconstruction. Looking southwards towards the sea, built from local limestone on a three-tier crepidoma, the temple was a relatively small construction measuring 31.87 x 15.12 meters. Its plan consisted of pronaos, cella and a very narrow (2 m deep) adyton whose floor was set lower than in the rest of the temple (Aupert 2000, 67). Four columns stood out from the façade, while the pilasters with carefully modelled bases were installed at the exterior corners of the temple wall and at two points near the back, marking the presence of the adyton wall (*Plate 2*). Capitals of columns and pilasters were in the so-called Nabataean style and were extremely well executed. Despite the fragmentary condition of their preservation, it is clear that the capitals from Amathous are of superior quality to those of Petra (cf. Aupert 2000, 69 and *Plate 3*). The decoration of other elements—architrave, frieze, and cornice—was simple without many floral decorations. The pediments were most probably not decorated at all. Systematic destruction of the temple makes an analysis of the interior design impossible, but it has been suggested that, like at Palaepaphos, the cult statue was in beatyl form (Hermary 2015, 39). The Aphrodite temple was the most spectacular building to transform the sanctuary on the Amathousian Acropolis, but its construction was not an isolated project of the Roman rebuilding phase (Aupert 2000, 69). The 1st century AD dedicatory inscription in Greek commemorates the construction of a stairway on the eastern side of acropolis at the expense of Loukios Vitellios Kallinikos (Aupert 1996, 108-109). The work included a vaulted gate at the summit that passed over the protective wall of the acropolis. The entrance to the sanctuary featured a small altar of Cypriote marble. Besides those new structures, earlier elements, including monumental vases (*Plate 3*), constituted the sacred landscape of the Amathousian sanctuary. Even without the evidence of Tacitus (Annales: 3.62 cited above) that placed the sanctuary in Amathous among the three most significant, the architecture of the temple of Aphrodite and scale of its construction activity alone would have ensured the major importance of this sanctuary in the religious life of the island in the Roman period. However, the most fully defined architectural complex at that time was, without any doubt, the sanctuary of Apollo Hylates (cf. Wright 1992, 167).

The sanctuary of Apollo worshipped as Hylates, the god of the woodlands, was located about 2.5 kilometres west of the ancient town of Kourion along the road which lead to Paphos. In the Hellenistic period, the site, enclosed by wall with two: Kourion and Paphos gates, consisted of a temple, a so-called Round Building, and an altar. Soren (1987, 35, 42) claims that the round building with pits cut into the bedrock for planting would have been filled with sacred trees but his arguments are far from convincing for Hunt (2016, 243), the author of the book *Reviving Roman Religion: Sacred Trees in the Roman World*. During the Roman period, the sanctuary was significantly re-built (*Figure 10*). A long doric portico extended the whole way between the two Kourian and Paphian gates. South of this portico, there was a structure consisting of five rooms

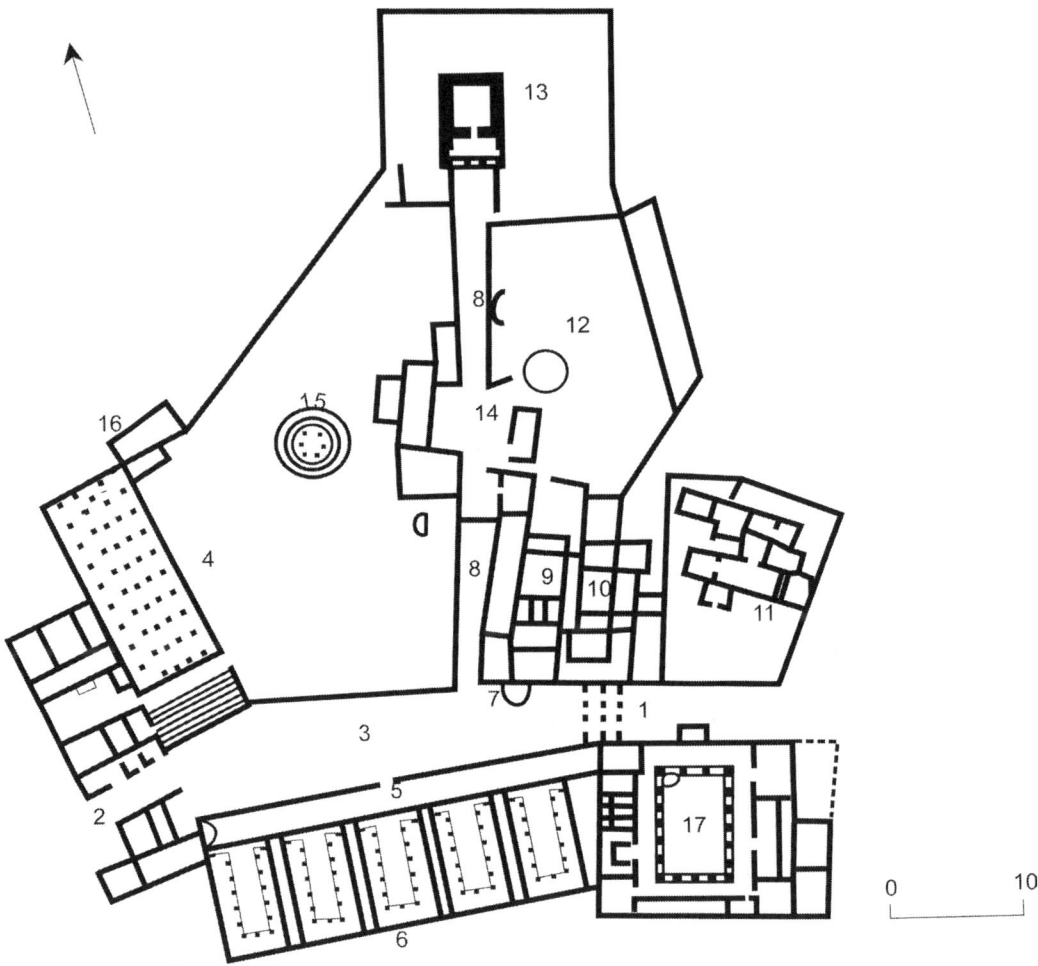

Figure 10. Plan of the Apollo Hylates Sanctuary—Roman phase – after Christou 1996, 67.
1. Kourion gate, 2. Paphos gate, 3. South court, 4. Northwest building, 5. Stoa, 6. South building, 7. Votive pit, 8. Central street, 9. Residence of the priest, 10. Treasury, 11. Baths, 12. Archaic precinct, 13. Temple of Apollo, 14. Central court, 15. Round Building, 16. Large cistern, 17. Palestra

separated from each other by corridors. The function of these rooms is not certain, but they may have been used to display votives or to accommodate visitors. The inscription set in the front wall over one of the doors informs that two of these rooms were erected by Trajan in 101 AD. To the North from the doric portico, a paved street leads directly to the temple of Apollo. The date for the first major temple dedicated to Apollo Hylates on site has been the subject of debate. It is certain though that at the end of the first/ beginning of the 2nd century AD, the Greek temple to Apollo Hylates was profoundly re-constructed (cf. Sinos 1990, 23). The temple built on a high stylobate consisted of a portico with four Nabatean columns, cella, and an adyton (*Plate 4*). Both the style of the structure (its plan, use of Nabatean capitals) and date of its construction point to the possibility that the temples of Apollo Hylates and Aphrodite of Amathous were both designed by the same team of architects (Hermary 1994, 328-9).

The Roman re-building phase also included work on the small building south of the precinct that may have been a priest's house. Along the external eastern side of the walls, palaestra and baths were erected. However, the main archaic elements—the Round Building and altar—seem to have remained unchanged. Although much of the building work was complete, the Roman contribution to the sanctuary mainly involved the modernizing and refining of existing areas while the ritually fixed division of sacred landscape did not change (Soren 1987, 39).

Salamis, Amathous, Kourion, the Greek model of a temple was introduced to all these important for Cypriote sanctuaries but it must be underlined that such structures remain extremely rare in Cyprus. Beside the aforementioned places, we possibly know one other structure from the Nea Paphos. The presence of the crepidoma suggested that the so-called Podium temple in the Ktisto area was a sacred building of the Greek type. Unfortunately, we do not even know the precise measurements of the structure as the north edge of stylobate is covered by the lighthouse substructure (Młynarczyk 1990, 202; *Figure 11*).

Fig 11. Nea Paphos—lighthouse. Photo by the author.

Decrease in religious activity?

Literary accounts, excavation reports, and survey projects (cf. The Sydney Cyprus Survey Project—Given and Knapp 2003, 2013) confirm that ex novo foundation of sanctuaries was extremely rare in the Roman Cyprus. A emperors' cult temple dedicated to Septimius Severus and Caracalla founded by the polis of Nea Paphos (Kantiréa 2008, 104) if existed (cf. Fujii 2013, 61) was unique.

Not much is known about sanctuaries located in the Roman poleis. Without any doubt, the temple of Aphrodite Paphia functioned in Nea Paphos. Her sanctuary was a gathering point for pilgrims and a place where the first stage of the ceremony was celebrated (Młynarczyk 1990, 22). Various sites have been suggested as a probable location for the temple, including Phanari and Fabrika Hill. The latter is more probable as several inscriptions referring to Aphrodite Paphia were found there (Karageorghis 2005, 61; Voros 2007). Beside the Podium temple and possible a sanctuary of Aphrodite Paphia in Fabrika Hill, in Roman Nea Paphos an underground sanctuary located in so-called Garrison's Camp—Toumballos area also functioned (*Figure 12*). Systematic research conducted by an Italian mission (Guidice et al. 2017, 771) uncovered a cut-in-rock complex consisting of a long dromos, a staircase leading downward, underground rooms and corridors. Due to the similarity to the Apollo Hylates hypogeum (see p. 32), it is often referred to as an Apollo sanctuary. However, taking into considerations the architectural plan, especially such elements as the presence of corridors and passages, as well as architectural features creating darkness, Młynarczyk (1990, 229-232) argues that the complex should be regarded as a cult place associated with chthonic beliefs, most probably of Egyptian origin.

Like in Nea Paphos, in Amathous too more than one sanctuary functioned. During excavation works performed in the agora area, the remains of two Roman temples have been found, although it is not clear to whom these structures were dedicated. Beyond the agora, a cultic installation dedicated to Aphrodite and Titus was located outside of the north gate of the city (Aupert and Hermary 2006; Aupert 2009 35-39).

Urban sanctuaries active in the Roman period are also reported in the Soloi acropolis, Keryneia and Kition. The archaeological (Soloi) and epigraphical material is far from rich, and we lack any evidence after the Severian dynasty.

The picture of inland sanctuaries is even more complicated. Cypriote temenoi traditionally had very limited architectural embellishment if any at all (Rupp 2000, 1095). If inscriptions are absent the sacred character of the site is often attributed based on the presence of terracotta figurines and /or fragments of limestone statuettes, sometimes very limited in number. As many sacred places in Cyprus are known from survey alone, it is difficult to recognize the exact picture of religious activity in the inland regions of the island. Recent excavation works conducted in Idalion demonstrated that sanctuaries located in Moutti tou Arvili hill and the so-called City Sanctuary still functioned in Roman period. The sanctuary of Adonis at Moutti tou Arvili was not only active till at least the middle Roman period but also, like sacred costal places, was significantly rebuilt and rearranged (Graber 2008, 59). Urban sanctuaries and shrines must have also functioned in Chytroi, Tamassos, and possibly in Ledra. However, it seems that none

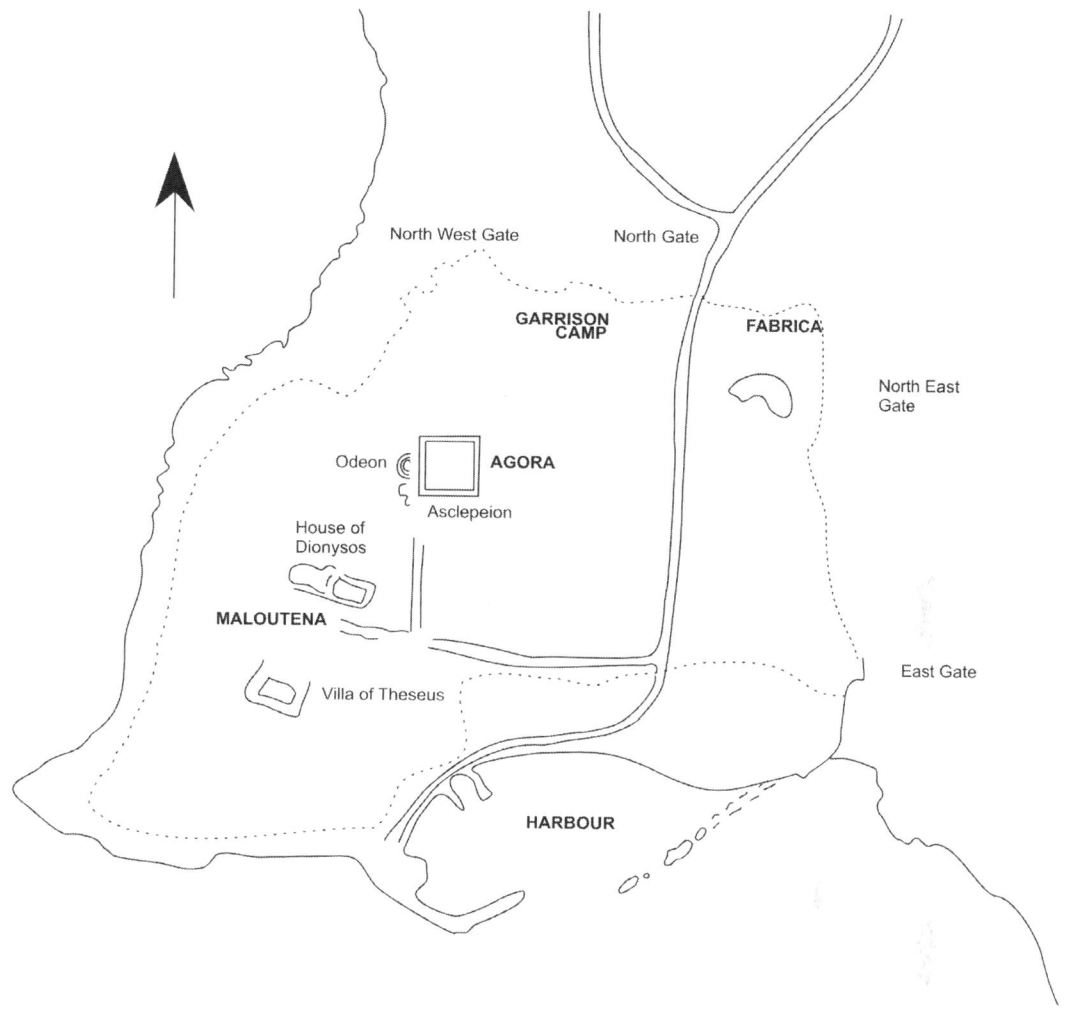

Figure 12. Plan of Nea Paphos: Maloutena, Agora, Fabrica Hill and Garrison's Camp. Sketch based on Rowe 2004, Figure 9.

of the inland sanctuaries were rebuilt under imperial patronage. Moreover, excavation reports indicate that the use of existing sanctuaries, especially extra-urban ones, was visibly reduced. Such important sites as Arsos, Voni—sanctuaries with age-old traditions of installing hundreds of limestone sculptures—are devoid of marble. On the other hand, some of the so-called rural sanctuaries like temenos of Opaon Melanthios at Amargetti, north of Palaipaphos (Masson 1994), Apollo at Louroudjina, and Apollo at Pyla (Mitford 1980, 1372) were active until at least the Severian period. The best-known example of a surviving rural cult is the hill-top sanctuary of Zeus Labranios at Phasoula (in the mountain region above Amathous) where tradition of portrait statuettes still occurred as late as the fourth century AD (Hermary 1992, 333-337).

RELIGION

The main Olympian gods

The Olympian gods: Hera, Artemis, Apollo, Demeter visibly appear both in archaeological material, mainly on coinage of the city—kingdoms, and in the epigraphic record in the late 5th century BC. At the beginning of the 4th century BC, most of the Cypro-Classical dynasties associated their lineage with Greek deities or heroes. At the same time, both the Cypriote basileis and Cypriotes also appear as dedicators in major Panhellenic sanctuaries (Papantoniou 2015, 2). The continuity of cult activity from the Cypro-Classical until the Ptolemaic period is confirmed by epigraphical material and the significant number of sanctuary sites that survived into Hellenistic times.

In opposition to other parts of the Roman East, Cyprus religious tradition during the Roman period did not change a lot. There was no Roman colonization on the island and Roman cults, apart from evidence of the cult of Roma, seem to have been insignificant. The Cypriote pantheon from the Hellenistic period is constant and very Greek in nature.

The Great Goddess Aphrodite

Greek and Latin literature celebrate Cyprus as an island of Aphrodite. Here, according to Hesiod Theogony (190-200), the sea-born goddess set her foot on land for the first time (*Plate 5*). The island was assigned as her terrestrial home and a prominent place of her cult. Aphrodite in Cyprus was named the Lady of the island (Πότνια Κύπρου), its Queen and Princess. Her rank differs much from the conventional mythological image of the blonde goddess of love, grace, and beauty. The Aphrodite of Cyprus was an ancient, powerful, universal divinity, the Cypriot goddess—Kypris. Excavations have yielded a vast amount of archaeological material which attested to the raising importance of her worship through the centuries as well as different images of the goddess. The history of the Aphrodite cult in Cyprus is particularly complex. Furthermore, there is no consensus among scholars concerning the exact relations of Greek, Phoenician, and local elements involved in the origins of Aphrodite worship in Cyprus (Benett 1980, 274). From the few early inscriptions available (6th century BC), we know that first the goddess was simply called η θεά—the Goddess. The epigraphical record indicates that the Goddess first began to be called Aphrodite in Amathous. However, it was the sanctuary in Paphos that remained the most ancient, most significant, and most famous place of Aphrodite's worship (*Plate 6*). According to Hesychius (Alexandrini lexicon s.v. *ómphalos*), a Greek lexicographer of the 5th century AD, Paphos together with Delphi were the omphalos—the central points of the terrestrial world believed to allow direct communication with the gods. The literary accounts (e.g. Homeric Hymn: 5. 58-65; Virgilius, Aeneida: 1.415-417; Tacitus, Histories: 2.3-4; Chariton, Callirhoe: 8.2.7-9) include the same information about the cult practices in Paphian sanctuary. It seems that from Late Bronze Age, the goddess was always presented in an aniconical form, as a sacred cone—baetyl. Just as the cult statue, the baetyl could either be a symbol of a goddess, have her powers or represent the goddess herself. Ancient writers were intrigued by this conical representation. Tacitus in Histories 2.3 noted:

> *The representation of the goddess is not in human form, but it is a circular mass that is broader at the base and rises like a turning-post to a small circumference at the top. The reason for this is obscure.*

As an important part of the local tradition, the sacred cone from Aphrodite sanctuary was depicted on Roman coins issued in the time between Augustus and Philip the Arab (cf. Maier 1975, 70 and *Figure 6*). In the Kouklia Museum, there is a baetyl from the Paphian Sanctuary II *(Plate 6)* which unfortunately had not been found in situ. Another peculiarity of the Paphian sanctuary was the fact that offerings to Aphrodite were never bloody. Tacitus (Histories: 2.3) emphasized that *Blood may not be shed upon the altar, but offering is made only with prayers and pure fire.* Indeed, despite its celebrity, the Roman sanctuary in Paphos yielded few votive offerings, including miniature models of altars, temples, and votary olive lamps *(Plate 6)*. Some fragments of crude limestone statues and terracotta statuettes were also noted.

The ceremonies honouring Aphrodite were very likely accompanied by music and dances (Karageorghis 2005, 58). Once a year, a panegyrical festival was organised as Strabo in Geographica 14 6.3 noted:

> *It is sixty stadia distant from Palæpaphus by land; and on this road men together with women, who also assemble here from the other cities, hold an annual procession to Palaepaphus.*

The existence of an oracle that was still consulted in Roman times is confirmed by both Tacitus and Swetonius (cf. Tacitus, Histories: 2.4; Swetonius, De vita Caesarum Titus: 5).

Perhaps mysteries celebrating some secret about the birth of Aphrodite were also organised. As the references to these mysteries are all from Christian authors (Clement of Alexandria, Hortatory: 2.12-13; Firmicus Maternus, De errore profanorum religionum: 10 and Arnobius, Adversus nationes: 5.19.2), it is possible that they were introduced in the late Roman period. In religious practices associated with Aphrodite—Kypris, scholars tend to highlight strong influence of pure oriental elements. It must be underlined, however, that in case of the Paphian sanctuary, it not so easy to point them out. There are no texts that specifically refer to oriental rites such as sacred marriage. Even if Christians authors very strongly underlined the immorality of Aphrodite's Cyprian cult, there is also no explicit mention about sacred prostitution. Compared with Palaipaphos, many more oriental rites and connotations are visible in another Aphrodite sanctuary—sanctuary at acropolis of Amathous.

Acropolis of Amathous (*Plate 7*), a city where according to sources (cf. Hipponax: 125-126) indigenous Cypriotes, who kept the Eteocypriote language alive, was an important place where the cult of the goddess was venerated, possibly as early as in the 11th century BC.

Tacitus in Annales (3.62—the whole passage cited above) noted that the people from Cyprus made claims for three shrines *the oldest erected by their founder Aerias to the Paphian Venus; the second by his son Amathus to the Amathusian Venus* (...) That passage confirms not only the importance of the Amathous' temple but also its antiquity as its founder was the son of Aerias—founder of (Palai)Paphos. The temple that Tacitus refers to is certainly a sanctuary situated on the top of the acropolis. In 70–100 AD, after the earthquake, it was rebuilt as a Greek-style temple with some visible oriental elements (see p. 21). The oriental elements are also noticeable in the cult of Aphrodite herself. From the Hellenistic period, the goddess was worshipped together with Isis. Outside Egypt, the greatest number of Isis figurines have been reported at the site of Amathous, indicating how important the Aphrodite-Isis connection was. The Amathousian cult was strongly associated with rites of fertility, and Hellenistic inscription dating to the reign of Ptolemy IV informed about the sacrifice made for those who cultivated the land (Pirenne-Delforge 1994, 353-354). It is possible that this inscription refers to a sacrifice called *Karposis* which according to Hesychius (Alexandrini lexicon s.v. *Karposis*) was made to Aphrodite in Amathous. The few references concerning sexuality seem to emphasize the antiquity of the religious practice (Karageorghis 2005, 110). Hesychius (Alexandrini lexicon s.v. *Afroditos*) quoting the Amathousian historian Paion, noted that *in Cyprus the goddess was given the appearance of a man.* Although Paion attributes this androgynous character to the Cyprian goddess; in general, its origin pointed to the city of Amathous in particular (Karagheorghis 2005, 111). And when Catullus (68a.51-52) speaks about duplex Amathusia, he may also be referring to this peculiarity. The worship of a bisexual Aphrodite may go back to the very distant past. Late antique sources still refer to some 'immorali' rites that may have been practised in Amathous. Actae Barnabae (20-21) described that it was *a great multitude of Greeks in the temple in the mountain, low women and men pouring libations.* From Life of Saint Tychon (60.3), we known that pagan *men and women, holding the statue of Kypris with torches and incense burners were passing near holy church in full pagan delirium and dancing. When the saint heard them, he went out, with his clergymen, broke the idol and made them ashamed....* (cf. Karageorghis 2005, 88). The archaeological data, however, indicates that the temple on acropolis was not very active and it seems to have been derelict as early as from the 3rd century AD (Aupert 2000,70). While the lower city was developing at that time, it is possible that another Aphrodite sanctuary was active in the city during the late Roman period.

The third sanctuary of Aphrodite active in Roman period was in Soloi-Choldes. Here the goddess, under the influence of Greek-Egyptian syncretism strongly promoted during the Hellenistic period by the Ptolemis, was mainly worshipped as Isis. Strabo in Geography mentioned that at Soloi there was a sanctuary of Aphrodite and Isis. Most probably he described the complex of two temples—so-called temple B and C (see p. 17). Within this building, the statue of Isis has been found with a crescent above her head.

Besides Paphos, Amathous and Soloi, the Aphrodite cult is visible in many other sites of Roman Cyprus. She was worshipped as Aphrodite Paphia Παφία, and Golgia Γολγία. Under the second name from the Cyptiot Iron Age the goddess was worshipped in Chytroi, Achna, and Idalion (cf. Ulbrich 2010, 170-171).

Among other epithets of the goddess known from Roman times, Aphrodite Akraia Ακραία occurs twice, first on the Oath of Allegiance which the Cypriots gave to the emperor Tiberius in 14 AD and in an inscription found near Rizokarpasso (Solomidou-Ieronymidou 1985, 62). That second inscription is probably associated with a sanctuary which foundations can still be seen on a plateau of a hill next to the Monastery of Apostolos Andreas (Karageorghis 2005, 198). This sanctuary was described by Strabo (14.6.3) as not to be visited and not to be seen by women and attributed by him to Aphrodite Akraia.

Apollo

The cult of Apollo in Cyprus is somehow parallel to that of Cypriote Aphrodite (Bennett 1980, 326). There are several known Cypro-Syllabic dedications found in Kourion (Mitford 1971, 38-42 = I. Kourion nos. 14-15), Golgoi-Hagios Photios (Masson 1983, 288), and Rantidi (Mitford and Masson 1983, 34-35) addressed to the god τῶ θεῶ. The name of Apollo was introduced under the Greek influence. The first Cypriote dedication to Apollo known so far is a 5th century BC votive inscription coming from the Kourion (Mitford 1971, 46-48 = I. Kourion no. 18). This text is carved on the plinth of a typical ex-voto temple boy. In bilingual Cypro-Syllabic/Phoenician dedications like this one from Idalion-Moutti tou Arvili the god is named both as Apollo and Semitic god Reshef (Teixidor 1983, 251-255; Graf 2009, 112-113). The iconography of votary statuettes depicts the divinity following both Greek (beardless kithara player wearing a laurel crown) and oriental (bearded, seated on a throne figure holding a sceptre) iconographical models. Under the Ptolemies, the Hellenised version of Apollo iconography became the dominant one (Hermary, 2009, 136-142).

The cult of Cypriote Apollo continued well into the Roman period. Perhaps the best know Apollo sanctuary is Kourion where from at least the 8th century BC Apollo was venerated under the local epithet Ὑλάτης Hylates. The epithet Hylates refers to the ancient divinity whose presence was experienced in the sacred wood-hyle constituting the temenos. Apollo Hylates is known not only from Kourion—he occurs also on dedications from others Cypriote sites: Nea Paphos (see p. 32), Dhrymou (village, in the district of Paphos) and Chytroi (Solomidou-Ieronymidou 1985, 63) The sanctuary in Kourion developed over time from a simple open-air site to an elaborate complex. The Roman temenos covered an area of about a hectare and included a temple, round building, altar, bath, palaestra, and associated buildings. (see p. 21-23). Unfortunately, not much is known about the rituals and beliefs connected with Apollo Hylates. Literary evidence is limited to the mentions by Strabo and Aelian. Strabo (14.6.3) informs that the sanctuary altar could not be touched on penalty of death. Aelian (De natura anima: 11.7) points to the existence of a custom according to which ...*when the deer (of which there are a great number and many hunters keen in pursuit of them) take refuge in the temple of Apollo there (the precinct is of very wide extent), the hounds bay at them but do not dare to approach.* The precinct to which Aelian refers in the quote is post probably located in the area of the so-called West Enclosure and, according to Soren (1987, 42), it might have functioned as a sort of sacred animal preserve. Such a hypothesis, however, should be verified by more precise research. Archaeological works offer some more details about the functioning of the sanctuary. The Archaic altar (*Plate 8*) was located north of the stoa within a precinct enclosed by wall (Soren 1987, 29). Research conducted by Diana Buitron and Giraud Foster demonstrates that the altar was used for animal sacrifices since at least 600 BC. The whole area was rich in sheep/goat bones, some cut for eating (Soren 1978, 28; 303). An inscription (Mitford 1971,195-199 = I. Kourion no. 104) refers to dancing around the sacred altar. Next to the altar, Scranton (1967, 7) located a large ashlar stone with a roughly rectangular hole which, according to D. Buitron and D. Soren (1980, 26-28; fig.5a), may have been a sacred baetyl. It seems that rites practiced at Kourion involved strong Near Eastern connections including the worship baetyls, sheep/goat sacrifices, and ring dancing (Soren 1987, 43). One of the special characteristics is the relation of the god with the nature, plants (some scholars claim that within the Round Building [cf. *Plate 8*] sacred trees were planted) and animals, which seems to be an essential component of the Cypriote Apollo character (cf. Vernet 2011, 251-264).

An interesting element of the cult of Apollo in Kourion is the cult of Apollo Caesar that occurred at least during the reign of Trajan in the early 2nd century AD. In this context, a monument dated to AD 101, which commemorated the completion of two exedrae to the gods Apollo Hylates and Apollo Caesar, is extremely important (Mitford 1971, 207-211= I.Kourion, no. 108 and *Figure 13*).

Figure 13. The inscription referring the construction of two exedrae in sanctuary of Apollo Hylates during the reign of Emperor Trajan. Episcopi museum. Photo by the author.

Αὐτοκράτωρ Καῖσαρ θεοῦ Νερούα υἱός Νερουας Τραϊανὸς Σεβαστὸς Γερμανικός ἀρχιερεὺς μέγιστος δημαρχικῆς (leaf)
ἐξουσίας τὸ δ΄ ὕπατος τὸ δ΄ πατὴρ πατρίδος τὰς λειπούσας ἐξέδρας δύο Ἀπόλλωνι Καίσαρι καὶ Ἀπόλλωνι Ὑλάτη(ι) ἔκτισεν· (leaf)
Κόιντος Λαβέριος Λουκίου υἱός Αἰμιλία Ἰοῦστος Κοκκεῖος Λέπιδος ἀνθίπατος τῆς κατασκευῆς ἐπεμελήθη καὶ καθιέρωσεν. L δ΄

Translation: Imperator Caesar son of the Deified Nerva, Nerva Trajan Augustus Germanicus, pontifex maximus, holder of tribunician power for the fourth time, consul for the fourth time, pater patriae, founded the two incomplete exedrae to Apollo Caesar and Apollo Hylat. Q(uintus) Laberius son of L(ucius), of the voting-tribe Aemilia, Iustus Cocceius Lepidus, proconsul, was responsible for the construction and dedicated them. In the fourth year.

According to Mitford (1990, 2184-5), the inscription indicated that the worship of Apollo Hylates and Apollo Caesar began during the reign of Trajan and the deity of Apollo Caesar represented the worship of this Roman Emperor. However, others (cf. Fujii 2013, 62-4; Kantiréa 2008, 101; 2010 269-271) highlighted that because the inscription describes the exedrae as already dedicated to Apollo Hylates and Apollo Caesar and completed only, thus implying that the introduction of the worship of Apollo Caesar probably antedated Trajan reign. Up to now, Apollo Caesar and Apollo Hylates appear on eight monuments. How and where Apollo Caesar was worshipped is ambiguous. Some scholars proposed that divided cella of the Northwest Building was a cultic place for both deities Apollo Hylates and Apollo Cesar. Although the cults of Apollo Hylates and Apollo Caesar were the most visible, they did not exhaust all the aspects of Apolline worship in Kourion region. In an inscription found at Kolossi near Kourion, Apollo is mentioned as the guardian of public roads—Agyates (Karageorghis 1998, 190).

Nothing is known about chthonic elements which could have been an important part of the Hylates cult in Kourion. However, two inscriptions, still in situ, indicate that Apollo Hylates was the titular divinity of the underground sanctuary in Alonia tou Episkopou—Nea Paphos (Masson 1983, 96-99, Młynarczyk 1980, 239-240). The specific architecture of this sanctuary and its location link directly the cult of Apollo Hylates with some chthonic rites (Młynarczyk 1980, 246-247). Another peculiarity of Apolline cult in Nea Paphos region comes from Amargetti sanctuary (see below p. 51-52). One dedication to Apollo Melanthios known from that site attested to the identification between the Olympian god Apollo and local deity Opaon (Mitford 1946, 38).

Beside the city of Kourion and Nea Paphos region, the cult of Apollo is especially well-proven in the Mesaoria plain. This region has been recognized as a Cypriote centre of this god (Vernet 2016, 354). By the end of the Hellenistic period, his worship is associated with twelve sites; among them, the god is clearly identified by dedications in Tamassos-Frangissa, Golgoi-Hagios Phôtios, Lefkoniko-Ayia Zoni, Chytroi-Skali and Voni. The sculpture is another key element to detect the religious presence of Apollo at Tamassos-Politiko, Malloura, Styllos-Krines and probably at Pyroi-Elia. At least some of above-mentioned sanctuaries (Golgoi-Hagios Phôtios, Chytroi-Skali, Voni, Malloura,

Pyroi-Elia) were still active in the early Roman period. The ritual activity in the Apolline temenoi of the Mesaoria Plain is not well recognised. Most of the sanctuaries belong to the extra-urban/rural types dated from the Cypriote Archaic period. The standard offerings were both bearded and beardless male statuettes. The god was often represented with wreaths of plants with medicinal attributes. Besides the plants, the laurel of Apollo was the most recurrent one (Cassimatis 1982, 156-163). This kind of ex-voto was also certainly involved in some rituals held to invoke regenerative divine forces for the fertility of the vegetation (Vernet 2015). A quite different aspect of Apollo cult is visible in Pyla-Stavros sanctuary (in region of Larnaca) where Apollo was worshipped under the epithet Mageirios. This epithet most probably related to the mageiroi, those who performed the sacrifices (Bennett 1980, 184). Little is known about this sanctuary itself. Both syllabic and alphabetic inscriptions indicate that in Pyla, he shares the sanctuary with his sister Artemis. Several limestone statues of Artemis were found in the sanctuary. Stylistically, they dated primarily to Hellenistic period and represented the goddess in a Greek form as a huntress; Artemis' right hand is usually placed on the head of a small stag which is standing by her feet. Her left arm is stretched down beside her body like in that statue dated to early Imperial period (Karagheorgis 1998, 180).

Zeus

Zeus was the main god of Salamis which, according to the Greek orator Isocrates (Evagoras: 50), was the most Greek among the cities of Cyprus. Indeed, the inscriptions dated to the 1st and 2nd centuries AD indicate that in Salamis, the god was worshipped under the well-known Greek epithet Olympios (Karageorghis 1998, 90). Unfortunately, despite the importance of the sanctuary that had the right of asylum, very little is known about the rites and the character of the worship of Zeus at Salamis. Between the main sanctuaries of Cyprus, this temenos was the only one located just inside the city next to agora. Excavations done by French mission have revealed that the first phase of construction of the temple took place in the late Hellenistic period. In these phase, the structure has been built as a spacious peripteral hexastyle temple with Corinthian columns (Argout et al. 1975, 138 see also p. 20). The cult statue of the god was represented on coins issued by the koinon of Cyprus. The god is depicted standing with a libation bowl in the right hand, an eagle perched on the sceptre *(Figure 14)*. Inscriptions attest the existence of a high priest of his cult.

Figure 14. The coin with Zeus Salaminos representation.

Besides Salamis, the cult of Zeus is also attested by other Roman poleis. The largest city of northwest Cyprus, Arsinoë, is credited by Strabo (14.6.3) with a sanctuary of Aphrodite and Zeus that most probably were active from the Archaic period into the early empire. Epigraphic evidence indicates the existence of a cult of Zeus Κεραύνιος, in Roman Kiton (Solomidou-Ieronymidou 1985, 61). Ten inscriptions on the statue bases found on the top Kastros hill about 1 km south-west of the village Phasoula refer to Zeus Λαβράνιος (Hermary 1992). Although the first two inscriptions were found as early as 1874 /1875, the site has never been a subject of systematic archaeological works. Many fragments of sculptures of Zeus dated to the 2nd and 3rd century AD were noted at the same place and it is highly probable that the inscriptions are fragments of statues representing Zeus himself. Two other dedications to Zeus Labranios are known from Chandria, a site located in the Trodos Mountains. One of those inscriptions is dated to the end of reign of Commodus.

Other Olympian gods

Other than those of Aphrodite, Apollo, and Zeus cults of Olympian gods in Roman Cypriot seem to have been mostly of local importance.

Artemis

It is agreed that Artemis was introduced to Cyprus during the 5th century BC along with other Greek gods and she was venerated under various epithets known from elsewhere. During the Hellenistic period, the local limestone statuettes and statues show that the images of Artemis were dedicated in various Cypriot sanctuaries, Pyla, Arsos, Idalion, Achna (Wriedt Sørensen 2009, 204; Karageorgis 1998, 176-186). However, she does not seem to have been the principal god of any of those sanctuaries. During the Roman period the goddess, together with her brother Apollo, was still worshipped in Pyla (see above p. 33), Malloura (Counts, Toumazou 2003) and, as epigraphical evidence indicates, also in Pera near Tamassos (Ulbrich 2008 546-553). The cult of Artemis Paralia in Salines near Kition has been the subject of a long academic debate. There are three dated to the late 2nd century AD dedications to Artemis Paralia. All these inscriptions were found around 1870 and presented by Luigi P. di Censola as coming from Larnaca Salt Marsh. Two of the dedications are now in the Metropolitan Museum of Art in New York while the third one—the dedication of Aurelios Ariston—is stored in Cabinet des Medallions in Paris. Where they were found — Larnaca Salt Marsh, Salines — made it possible to locate the sanctuary of Artemis Paralia in the north part of the salt lake (*Plate 9*) in the same place where a deposit of terracotta figurines dated to 5th-4th century BC was found (Yon 1992, 301). As there is a significant chronological gap between the deposit of statuettes and the epigraphical records, this connection was questioned many times but it was not excluded. The Artemis Paralia seems to be a deity deeply rooted in the environment and cultural landscape of ancient Kition. The same epithet Paralia was also present in the fourth epigraphical record. Unfortunately, this inscription is only known from a description and drawing presented by Alessandro Palma di Censola in his book Salaminia (1882, 96; fig.105 cf. *Figure 15*). Both Nicolaou (1976, 111) and Mitford (1957, 164) suggested a possible confusion regarding where it was found between Salamis and Kition. However in Salamis, like in Kition, salt production was active during the whole Roman period so this second possible place of worship of Artemis Paralia cannot be overruled. From at least the period of reign of Pnytagoras, (351–331 BC) who chose to use the

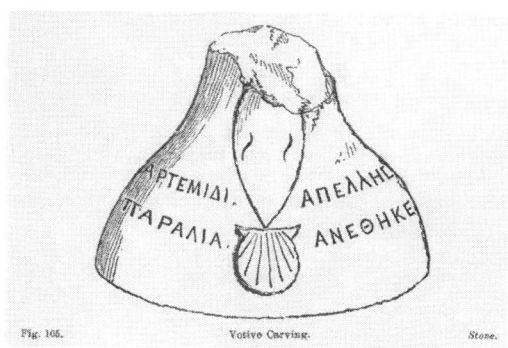

Figure 15. Dedication to Artemis Paralia—drawing based on Censola 1882, fig. 105.

representation of Artemis as an emblem on the reverse of silver didrachmae, Salamis was especially linked with the goddess. Two fragmentary preserved early Roman marble statues from the Salaminian gymnasium are the most impressive images of Artemis known from Cyprus. They are both dated to the 2nd century AD and depicted the goddess as a hunter according to the so-called Laphria and Versailles types, respectively (Wriedt Sørensen 2009, 200).

The worship of another important Olympian goddess—*Athena* is attested only to the two main Roman Cypriote cities, Nea Paphos and Salamis. According to an inscription dating to the 2nd century BC, there was a sanctuary of Athena in Salamis (Karagheorghis 1998, 170). This sanctuary probably functioned until late period as Porphyrios (De Abstinentia: 2.54) mentioned a peribolos wall which enclosed the sanctuaries of Athena, Agraulos, and Diomedes. The Salamis gymnasium was adorned with a marble statue of the goddess, a copy of the so-called Athena Hephaesteia type, which had been created by Alkemenes for a temple in Athens. This statue found in 1890 is now located in Ashmolean Museum of Oxford (Karageorghis and Vermeule 1966, 13 f.).

Besides the constant presence of Artemis and Athena in the religious landscape of Cyprus, there were also cults of *Hera* who was worshipped as the spouse of Zeus. According to Bennett (1980, 125), in Amathous there was a Heraion where every year Amathousians celebrated the marriage of Hera and Zeus—a ritual connected with the fertility of fields, animals, and humans. The only known representation of Hera in Cyprus is a colossal marble statue found in gymnasium of Salamis (Karageorghis and Vermeule 1964, 35 f.).

The cult of the goddess *Hestia* under the epithet Βουλαία is confirmed by the Oath of Allegiance and an inscription from the Roman period, found in the village of Nikokleia, near Palaipaphos (Solomidou-Ieronymidou 1985, 60). A Domitianic inscription names a high priestess of all temples of *Demeter* on the island, although their locations are unknown (Mitford 1980, 1371). Finally, the association of the cult of god *Asclepios* and that of the goddess *Hygiea*, is attested in Cyprus by only two epigraphical documents, one Hellenistic, found in the Sanctuary of Aphrodite at Palaipaphos, and one Roman, found at Dromolaxia village, in the district of Larnaca (Solomidou-Ieronymidou 1985, 59).

Oriental gods

The oriental element was consistently present as an integral part of local Cypriote beliefs.

Cults of Phoenician origin

The geographical proximity of Cyprus to the Near East was the primary reason for *longue durée* commercial relations between the two regions. The presence of the Phoenicians in Cyprus at the beginning of the 1st millennium BC was the continuation of those close commercial links. Salamis, Kition, Palaipaphos, and Chiorokitia are four locations on the island where Phoenician inscriptions dating before the 8th century BC were found. From the 7th century BC, the signs of Phoenician presence increased especially in the ports of Amathous and Kition as well as in Tamassos, Chytroi, and Idalion. At that time both Phoenicians and the Cypriotes had to deal with the rise of two empires—the Assyrian and then the Persian (Ioannou 2015). During the classical period, the Phoenicians, with Persian support, succeeded in establishing a dynasty in Kition. At a site known as Kathari (*Plate 9*), they built on the ruins of a sanctuary of a feminine deity, a temple dedicated to Astarte which was the largest temple of a goddess ever found in the Mediterranean (Karageorghis 2005, 113). The temple remained in use until the 4th century BC (Karageorghis 2005, 146). In the eastern part of the city—the Bamboula site—stood the temple where Astarte was worshipped together with Ball of Kition/Melqart who was the protector of the city also identified with Herakles. The temple continued to be used until the early Hellenistic period (Karageorghis 2005, 148-156). Also, the existence of a temple of the god Esmun-Melqart on the Patsalos Hill was confirmed by archaeological remains (Michaelidou-Nicolaou 1978, 796). The cult of Phoenician gods was found not only in Kition but also in Idalion, Tamassos, Larnaca tis Lapethon, and probably Amathous as Hesychios (s.v. Malika) refers to (Michaelidou-Nicolaou 1978, 797). With passing time, purely Phoenician elements were strongly influenced by Greek cults. Excavations in the last fourth phase of Astarte temple in Kition yielded terracotta and limestone statuettes in the purest Greek style (Karageorghis 2005, 146). After 312 BC, the main Phoenician temple seems to have been abandoned. In the Roman period, Phoenician cults remained a distant religious tradition.

Egyptian goods

The representations of Egyptian deities and semi gods (for example Bes figurines) are visible in Cyprus from at least Late Bronze Age (Michaelidou-Nicolaou 1978, 791). During the Cypro-Archaic period there is undoubted evidence of influence of Egyptian symbolism. A brief period of Egyptian rule (about 560 – 540 B.C) fostered Cypriote economic relations with Egypt. In the religious sphere elements such as the head of Hathor appeared in quantity for the first time especially at Amathous. The Hathor cult is also evidenced in the 6th – 5th century BC by imposing limestone capitals. They bear different Egyptian symbols like papyrus, sun disc or cobra. Also the representations of Osiris, Isis, Ptah and Anubis are well visible in cultic-related material. Although many figurines and statues of ram-headed god were also found at Cypriote sites Zeus Ammon is never mentioned by name (Bennett 1980, 479; Counts 2009, 112).

In the Ptolemaic period, a new wave of Egyptian influence is visible. During this period the cult of Egyptian gods was connected with the cult of the royal family (Bennet 1980, 479-480) and there was a visible tendency to legitimize authority through the manipulation of cults and sacred space (Papantoniou 2012, 361).

Serapis

Among the cults of Egyptian deities developed in Cyprus during the Ptolemaic period, that of Serapis seems to have been the earliest. His cult in Cyprus is attested epigraphically from the early 3rd century BC in Salamis and Soloi (Michaelidou-Nicolaou 1978, 797). The cult of Serapis forged Greek and Egyptian elements into something new, which appealed especially to the non-Egyptian subjects of the Ptolemaic kingdom. Primarily, the appearance of the god was Greek; the cult statue created by Bryaxis was to become the model of his representations. In addition, significant elements of the tradition of Greek cults of mysteries appear to have been incorporated into the rituals. On the other hand, many typically Egyptian priestly titles are connected to his cult (Pfeiffer 2008, 392-393). Serapis was then a god that may have supported identification with Egypt and its Ptolemaic dynasty as early as from the reign of Ptolemy II Ptolemeis, who actively attempted to participate in spreading the cult (Pfeiffer 2008, 398). The consistent presence of Serapis in Cyprus continued well into the Roman period. The excavations at Soloi-Cholades showed that a temple (Temple E) dedicated to Serapis (Westhlom 1936, 151-152) existed there in the Severian period. Probably to this temple belongs a sculpture of Serapis (*Figure 16*). Following Alexandrian traditions, he was depicted both as a god of fertility and the underworld. In the same temple, a cult-statue of god Canopus was found almost in its original position on the altar (Westholm 1936, 151; Vermeule 1976, 122). Kleibl (2007, 139-140) believes that the sculpture of Serapis was in fact part of a Serapis-Cerberus cultic group. The Serapis cult-related finds are also known from other Roman sites of Cyprus including Salamis, where at least one Bryxis-

Figure 16. Limestone head of Serapis from Soloi-Cholades. Cyprus Museum in Nicosia. Photo by the author.

type representation has been found, and Arsos. Two dedications found in Arsos: one on plaquette decorated with phallus, the second on votive colonnette (Masson 1980, 273-275; Hermary 1990, 45-49) attest to the worship of the famous Egyptian trinity Sarapis, Isis, and Anubis. In the context of significance of Serapis in the religious landscape of Roman Cyprus two more objects are worth mentioning here. One of them is the famous jasper gemme with a representation of seated Serapis placed next to the temple of Cypriote Aphrodite in Palaipahos (Petrie 1927, 19). Although the exact motives of such an association remain obscures (cf. Veymiers 2005, 355) this object of unknown provenance, point to an important influence of Egyptian elements onto to Cypriote believes The second find is a boat-shaped lamp found in Nea Paphos. The lamp dated to the $2^{nd}/3^{rd}$ century AD was decorated with deities of the Egyptian pantheon. Most of the deck of the boat was occupied by the representation of Serapis, while the formula HLEIO SERAPES was inscribed on the flat and undecorated base before the lamp was fired. It seems that a larger boat-shaped lamps, especially those with inscriptions, had a votary essence. The lamp from Nea Paphos pointed then to the introduction of syncretism Helios (Sol) and Serapis visible in other parts of Mediterranean. This new god, as a protector of travelling, was worshipped in various maritime and fluvial ports. It seems that in this case the Cypriote religious landscape reflects the growing significance of long-distance trade in the social life of the island (Michaelides 2009, 197).

Isis

Beside Serapis, the cult of Isis was an important element of Cypriote beliefs (Michaelidou-Nicolaou 1978, 798). It is primary visible in two Cypriote sites, Amathous and Soloi-Cholades. From the 2nd century BC in Amathous, the cult of Isis was connected to the cult of Aphrodite. Numerous figurines were found representing the goddess with such characteristic features as a knotted himation and Hathoric crown. Moreover, the inscriptions found at the site refer to the cult of Serapis, Isis, and associated gods (Karageorghis 2005, 105). In Soloi-Cholades, the cult of Isis was most probably venerated in so-called Temple C. A limestone statuette found just outside the cella is related, according to Westhlom (1936, 200), to the myth of Isis and Osiris

Figure 17. Limestone head of Isis from Soloi-Cholades. Cyprus Museum in Nicosia. Photo by the author.

known inter alia from Plutarch (Moralia: 5.351-384) and represents Isis kneeling on a column that contains the remains of her husband (Papantoniou 2012, 175).

The identification of Temple C as a cult place of Isis might be supported by textual evidence. Strabo (14.6.3) mentioned a sanctuary sacred to Aphrodite and Isis. At his time, temples B and C had probably replaced temple A, and among them, temple B was dedicated to Aphrodite and C to Isis, respectively. The presence of Isis in the temples at Cholades is also attested by other representations (*Figure 17*). Most of the sculptures of style II have been ascribed as related to Isaic iconography. The recent architectural analysis done by Kleibl (2007, 133-137) might also confirm the practice of Isaic cult in Temple D, which remained in use until the fourth century AD. Of course, the cult of Isis in the Roman period was not limited solely to Amathous and Soloi-Cholades. Two dedications from Arsos (see above p. 38) indicate the worship of the Egyptian trinity Serapis, Isis, and Anubis. It must be noted here that the cult of Anubis played a more important role on the Greek islands—for example, on Delos—than it seems to have had in Hellenistic Egypt; therefore behind the presence of the cult of that particular trinity seems to stand a more complicated process than the direct influence of official Ptolemias propaganda. The 'standard' Alexandrian Isis companion—Harpocrates—is represented in Cypriote on gold, glass, and bone objects. The images of the god can also be found on lamps and pendants but there is no evidence regarding his cult or the cult of Egyptian trinity (Sarapis, Isis and Harpocrates) as a unit (Michaelides 2009, 205).

Bes

Although the worship of the Egyptian god Bes is not attested in the epigraphy of Cyprus, the presence of this deity during the Roman period is also worth mentioning here. The god had a significant impact on the religious landscape of Amathous. The Egyptian Bes known in Amathous from at least the Cypro-Archaic period after many modifications seems to have become the local element of the consort of the Amathousa goddess (Papantoniou 2012,

Figure 18. Statue of Bes from Amathous. Archaeological museum in Istanbul. Photo by the author.

265). The discovery of several statues of the Egyptian god Bes, including a colossal one (*Figure 18*), suggests the high popularity of this deity in the Hellenistic period. Some representation of Bes found in Amathous can be also dated to the Roman period (Aupert 2000, 43).

Cult of Emperors

In the official and highly formulated texts such as the inscription on a milestone (*Figure 19*), the word theos was the Greek synonym of divus and reflected a political decision made in the capital regarding the consecration of the emperor (Fujii, 2013, 24). However, there was no one-to-one equivalence between the word theos and the Latin divi (Price 1984). In Cypriote inscriptions, emperors mentioned as theos are Caesar, Augustus, Tiberius, Nero, Vespasian, Nerva, Trajan, Hadrain, Septimios Severus, and Caracalla. The fact that Tiberius and Nero did not receive official consecration indicates that the term theos was used in a broader sense. Like in other eastern provinces, it included not only the divi consecrated by central government but also other emperors and imperial family members who were not given the title divus/ diva after their death. For example, the inscription from Palaipaphos named Iuia who died in exile as Iulia Thea Sebaste. In some ways, the worship of the Roman emperors and members of the imperial household reflects some of the practices observed during the Ptolemaic period. Another inscription from Palaiaphos, which named Livia as Thea Nea (Cayla 2004, 234-236), echoes the association of Ptolemaic Queens with local deities (cf. van Oppen de Ruiter 2007, 12-13). As Fujii underlines (2013, 159), traditional rituals and the royal cult of Ptolemeis provided the imperial cult in Cyprus with a frame of reference. There was a linear ideological continuation—the traditional form of cults continued in a different context. How the imperial cult was exactly arranged is not clear. It seems that the three types of imperial priesthoods revealed in the epigraphic record corresponded to three levels of imperial

Figure 19. A fragment of inscribed milestone. Cyprus Museum in Nicosia. Photo by the author.

cult—provincial, civic, and individual. The monopoly of the individual imperial cult must have been enjoyed by a select few families and limited to extremely wealthy people. One fragmentary inscription from Salamis refers to an emperor who held the seventh tribunicia potestas and the seventh acclamation of imperator when this inscription was set up. According to the general consensus (Mitford 1947, 220-22; Kantiréa 2008, 110; Fujii 2013, 28), this emperor was Nero. This was an individual dedication sponsored by the dedicator at his own cost and addressing the emperor as his own god.

Although there are some testimonies about the sanctuaries of Ptolemaic rulers in Cyprus, Arsinoeion in Idalion (Anastassides 1998, 138), Ptolemaion in Paphos (Mitford 1961a, 40-41), and possibly a temple for Arsinoe in Amathous (Flourentzos 2007), the independent temple or sanctuary founded specifically for an emperor's veneration is very rear if not, as Fujii (2013, 57) suggested, totally unconfirmed. As in the other eastern provinces, the cult of the emperor was introduced to the sanctuaries of traditional deities, although this practice seems not to have been very frequent. Two inscriptions from Amathous indicate a sanctuary of Aphrodite and Titus (see p. 24) We know also that in Kourion there was a cult of Apollo Hylates and Apollo Caesar (see p. 31-32). Two fragmentary inscriptions on a stone-like altar found near the gate of Salamis refer to Augustus as Zeus Caesar. There is also known an inscription that honours a certain Hyllos grand-priest of Zeus Olympios and Augusts (Kantirea 2008, 95; Yon 2009, 289, 291). Although it has been proposed that the temple of Zeus in Salamis housed the cults of emperors (cf. Yon 1980, 92-93; Yon 2009, 305), evidence is very scarce, and this inscription should not necessarily be linked with it. For the cult of emperors in others Cypriote sanctuaries, epigraphical testimonies are lacking. However, the concentration of statue base inscriptions in cultic places is remarkable. According to research conducted by Fujii (2015, 252), out of 28 dedications with details of their origins available, 21 are from religious sites. Imperial statues included monuments to emperors, empresses, as well as younger imperial family members, especially during the Julio-Claudian period. Unfortunately, we do not as yet have any representation dedicated to a Roman emperor with an inscription nor has any statue been found in situ. It is difficult then to distinguish between the religious-cultic and non-religious honorific representations of emperors found within the temenoi. The bronze statue of Septimius Severus from Chytroi (*Plate 10*) is almost the sole representative example of a naked representation of the emperor attested in Cyprus (Fujii 2015, 246). As a rule, the nudity of statues enhanced their divinity and is connected with a cult which seems to be also the case with the statue of Severus. Other statues seem to be honorific representations. Placing an imperial image in a sacred site is a widely accepted convention in the Roman Empire. The fact that there is no archaeological evidence in most of Cypriote sanctuaries pointing to the existence of structures built in order to accommodate the needs of an imperial cult, makes it quite probable that the imperial statues were put there alongside other images and votive offerings dedicated to the main deities of the sanctuaries (Fujii 2015, 253); this could made a dramatic change in the visual arrangement of the temenoi but with the material available such a possibility cannot be determined.

Religious and non-religious honorific monuments, plaques, and votives dedicated to the Roman Emperor were introduced not only to the sanctuaries but also the most visible places within the Cypriote cities. For instance, a statue base from Kourion (cf. Mitford 1971, 153-157 = I. Kourion no. 84) indicates the commemoration of cultic rituals at Kourion to Augustus and Nero. The erection of this statue was founded by Kourion, while the proconsul Iulius Cordus approved the additional expense, and another proconsul, Annius Bassus, performed rituals for setting up the statue (Fujii 2013, 54). The statues of emperors were also introduced to public buildings. The theatre of Salamis (*Plate 11*) accommodated both statuary portraits of Greek deities (Dionysos and Apollo with the Muses) and Roman emperors.

The incorporation of the worship of the emperor into the local game calendar is another characteristic element of cult of emperors in Roman Cyprus. A monument of Gaius Ummidius Durmius Quadratus discovered in Nea Paphos informs us about a festival for the Emperor known as the Neroneia. Another inscription celebrates an individual for acting as a voluntary agonothetes who supervised sacred contests known as the Kaisarogermanikeia (Fujii 2013, 128-129).

Cult of heroes

Foundation myths—Greek Heroes in literature and myths

The foundation myths of the Cypriote poleis were recorded over time by different ancient authors. According to them, many of poleis were foundations of Greek heroes, particularly heroes returning from the Trojan War. Lycophron's epic Alexandria alone give us names of five heroes returning from Troy that founded Cypriot cities: Teukros, Agapenor, Akamas, Cepheus and Praxandrus (lines 450-591). Einer Gjerstad (1944, 107) observed that the process of use and adaptation of Cypriot foundation myths generally reflected the colonisation of Cyprus and, in doing so, followed '*the usual Greek system used in reconstructing ethnic movements of earlier times*'. The relationship between the colonisation of Cyprus and the circulation of foundation myths has been closely examined by M. Fortin. The close overview trough an archaeological material led to the conclusion that the foundation myths of many Cypriote poleis, including Paphos, Kourion, Soloi (Fortin 1980), and Amathous (Fortin 1984), correspond to archaeological evidence (cf. Fourrier 2008).

Paphos

Ancient literature describes Palaipaphos as the site of Aphrodite's birth and her sanctuary. (Młynarczyk 1990, 23-35). Strabo in Geographica (14.6.3) briefly noted that the Greek hero Agapenor founded Paphos εἶθ' ἡ Πάφος, κτίσμα Ἀγαπήνορος. This version of foundation with more details was presented also by Pausanias (Hellados Periegesis: 8.5.2-3).

While Strabo and Pausanias indicated Agapenor as the founder of Paphos, Tacitus (Historiae: 2.3.1; Annales: 3.62.4) wrote about two different founders, king Aerias and Kinyras.

Tacitus wrote (Historiae: 2.3.1):

> Conditorem templi regem Aeriam vetus memoria, quidam ipsius deae nomen id perhibent. Fama recentior tradit a Cinyra sacratum templum deamque ipsam conceptam mari huc adpulsam; sed scientiam artemque haruspicum accitam et Cilicem Tamiram intulisse ...

> The founder of the temple, according to old tradition, was King Aerias. Some, however say that this was the name of the goddess herself. A more recent tradition reports that the temple was consecrated by Cinyras, and that the goddess herself after she sprang from the sea, was wafted hither; but that the science and method of divination were imported from abroad by the Cilician Tamiras......

Not much is known about the figure of King Aerias. Hero Kinyras, however, is far better known from written sources. He is presented as a local Cypriote or as a man originating from 'eastern lands' mainly from Cilicia, the place from where, according to Tacitus, Tamiras—who brought the sacred art of divination—came as well. Literary accounts (see Table 1) conflate the genealogy of Kinyras with other familiar mythological figures. For example, in Ovid's Metamorphoses (10.270-298), he is a descendant of Pygmalion. Even a superficial overview of the ancient literature demonstrates that Kirynias was a well-known figure both to Greek and Latin authors and he was traditionally associated with the Paphian sanctuary and with the goddess Aphrodite (cf. Baurain 1980). Beside his role as a founder of the sanctuary, Kirynias was also associated with establishing activities which were key to the identity of the island, such as copper mining and introducing tools for metallurgy.

Despite numerous mythological accounts of the importance of Kirynias in the religious landscape of Cyprus, archaeologically he is almost nowhere to be seen. In the current state of evidence, it is only the city's last king of Paphos, Nikokles II for whom we have any epigraphic evidence of the Kinyrad legacy (Franklin 2015, 409). An inscription most probably carved on the base of a statue dedicated to Paphian Aphrodite at Ledroi contains Kinyras name. Following the Mitford (1961b, 136-138) proposition, it can be translated as follows:

> I[n] the Ledrians' precinct of P[aphia, a scion of glorious]
> Fathers, Arkhaios, [admiringly erect]ed [sc. a statue of]
> Timarkhos' son, the Paphians' [outstanding king]-
> Nikokles, of div[ine-speaking] Kinyras [descendant].

The inscription paleographically dated to the last quarter of the fourth century is supremely important as proof confirming the Kinyrad monarchy at Paphos known from literary traditions (Clement of Alexandria, Protrepticus: 3.40). After the Ptolemaic annexation of Cyprus, the Kinyrades were dethroned, although it seems the title still remained in use. According to Tacitus (Historiae: 2.3), the office of priesthood in Paphos sanctuary became hereditary in the families of both Kinyras (Kinyradae) and Tamiras, but in the times of Tacitus, only the priest of the Kinyras line was consulted.

The only known epigraphical evidence utilising the association of Kinyras in the Roman period is an inscription discovered at the sanctuary of Paphian Aphrodite dating to the 2nd century AD (Hogarth et al. 1888, 249, no 101).

[Ὁ ερεὺς αφίας Ἀφρο]δίτης ? Διονυσό[δωρος] Διονυσίου Κινύραρ[χον]μου φιλοτειμίας καὶ ε g φι[λαγαθίας χάριν] τὸν πατέρα

Translation:
[The priest of Paphian Aphro]dite ? Dionyso[dorus the son of Dionysus Kinyrar[chin] recognition of his zeal and [his benevolence], the father.

The fact that no other evidence survived from Roman Cyprus of this title, does not mean that Dionysodorus and his father were the only individuals named as kinyrarch. The way how this 'ancient' local title is included in inscription indicated that it still was a prestigious one and important for personal identity.

The detailed study of the Oath of Allegiance to Tiberius done by Cayla (2001, 69-81) suggested that a hero cult to Kinyras existed in the Paphos region during the Roman period. Cayla's interpretation of the monument was that the inscription was drafted exclusively by the city of Paphos and that the possessive adjective hemeteros identifies the deities as local and specific to the Paphos region. In that context, a particular interest of the Cayla study is the identity of Apollo. Instead of Apollo Keryneia, a new reading of the epithet of Apollo as Κε[ν]υριστην is suggested. In this point of view, Kinyras, a founder of Paphian sanctuary, was syncretized with the main Cypriote male god Apollo and worshipped in the Paphos region as a 'double hero'. Such an interpretation is very attractive because ancient literature often placed Kinyras alongside Apollo and confirms the 'double' (deity with heroic epithet) cult of Ariadne-Aphrodite (see p. 51) in the Cypriote context too. It seems, however, that Cayla's proposition remains only a speculation without any archaeological proof. As Fujii (2013, 80) and others underline, Aphrodite Akraia, Kore, Apollo Hylates, and the Dioskouroi, all are deities that were not specific to Paphos and have been venerated across the island.

The identification of three founders of the Paphos: King Aerias, Kinyras, and Agapenor demonstrate the flexibility in shaping the mythology of the polis and sanctuary (Hussein 2014, 196). During the Roman period, it is the mythology of Kinyras and his descendants that is visible in a cultic context. The presence of Kinyras among the foundation rites of Paphos could have highlighted the eastern associations of the sanctuary. The role of hero, however, was reduced solely to the traditional eponymous of the local priest collegium and without any doubt had little impact on the religious landscape of the region.

Salamis

Salamis was a foundation of the Greek hero Teuker (cf. Isocrates, Evagoras: 18; Horacy, Carm: 1.7.21-29; Pausanias, Hellados Periegesis: 8.15.5-7). Similar to the hero Kinyras of Palaipaphos, the figure of Teuker was important to the kings of Salamis. To legitimate their power and status, they claimed their descent from Teuker (cf. Antoninus Liberalis,

Table 1. Genealogy of Kinyras.

		Bion 1.91-92	Ovid Met 10.220-550	Apollodorus Bibliot 3.14.3-4	Josephus AJ 19.91-97	Plutarch Mor 311.A	Hyginus Fab 142.4	Athenaeus 10.456 a-b	Stephanus Amathous, Kypros, Kurion, Marion	Hesychius s.v.Kinyras
Father	Sandocus			V						
	Paphos						V			
	Apollo									V
Mother	nymph Paphia		V							
	Pharnace			V						
	Amathousa								V	
Wife	Cencheris		V							
	Methame daughter of Pygmalion			V						
Son	Adonis	V	V				V			
	Oxyporos			V						
	Koureus, Marieus								V	
	Braesia, Laogore Orsedice			V						
Daughter	Laodice			V (3.14)						
	Myrrha				V					
	Cyprus								V	
	Smyrna				V	V				

Arkeophon: 39.1-6; Bennet 1980, 472). However, in the Roman period, it appears that the myths of Teuker were not relevant in any significant way and did not shape the religious landscape of the city.

Literary and mythological references to Akamas, Amathous, Golgos suggest the possibility that they were worshipped in their respective cities. There is no, however, evidence for cults of these eponymous heroes of any of Cypriote polis (Bennet 1980, 269).

Kourion

The foundation of Kourion is recorded in a variety of sources, dating from the 5th century BC to the 5th century AD (Herodotus, Historiae: 5.113.1; Strabo, Geographica: 14.6.3, Stephanus Byzantius, Ethnica: 380. 4-6). The ancient writers claim that the city was a foundation/colony of the Argives (for Herodotus cf. Lavelle 1984). The epigraphical evidence points to hero Perseus, a son of Zeus and Danaë, the daughter of Acrisius, king of Argos, as the founder of the city. Inscriptions discovered in Kourion (Mitford 1971, 60-62; 128-129 = I. Kourion, nos. 25, 65, 66) signal the worship of Perseus, Perseutas mainly in the pre-Roman period. According to Mitford (1971, 128) there must have been a temenos dedicated to the hero, most probably situated upon the Acropolis. This temenos seems to have existed in late Classical/early Hellenistic period. With passing time, the cult of Perseus was stifled by the worship of Apollo Hylates and did not survive into the Roman period. However, Bagnall and Drew-Bear (1973, 219), in their commentary on The Inscriptions of Kourion, call into question the Hellenistic dating of inscriptions nos. 65 and 66 and whether the sanctuary of Apollo Hylates would have stifled the worship of hero. It seems that in the Roman period, Kourion still continued to style itself as a city of Perseus.

A fragmentary marble tablet, discovered at the sanctuary of Apollo Hylates (Mitford 1971, 195-199 = I. Kourion no. 104) dated to 130/131 AD, and set up by a Roman official, marks a local response to the death of Antinoos, lover of the Emperor Hadrian. The inscription records the introduction of a festival for Antinoos into the Cypriot calendar. In line thirteen, we can find Perseus' name. That fragment can be read as the reference to the foundation of Kourion city which sprung from the blood of Perseus (τὸ Φορωνικὸν αἷμα τὸ ερσέως οι). According to the above-mentioned inscription, it could be argued that not only the reference to Perseus but also the composition of this hymn in the Doric dialect highlighted Kourion's Argive foundation.

On the honorific slab of marble discovered in sanctuary of Apollo Hylates (Mitford 1971, 165-167 = I. Kourion no. 89), we can read:

> οπλικόλαν ρεῖσκόν με
> πόλις ερσῆος ἄγαλμα
> κοίρανον ἁγνείας
> στήσατο παρ' τεμένει

Translation:
The city of Perseus set up me,
Publicola Priscus, a statue
the leader of holiness,
in the temenos.

This honorific slab was possibly fixed onto a pedestal bearing the statue of Publicola Priscus, possibly a Roman proconsul or administrative official. Although the dating of the monument is not fixed, it was most probably erected at the end of the 3rd century AD as the features of the text render it typical of the Second Sophistic movement (Hussein 2014, 212). As in the earlier inscriptions, Kourion is still named as a city of Perseus.

Neither archaeological nor literary sources link Perseus with Kourion or attest to his worship in the polis. This seems to suggest that the connection between the demigod and the city was only expressed epigraphically. In in the Greco Roman world, it was not uncommon for cities to claim a link with a god or hero to enhance their status and to underline their Greek identity.

From Oriental god to a Greek hero

Herakles

The roots of the cult of Herakles in Cyprus are obscure. Many of the local cults are probably Hellenized versions of Phoenician Melqart worship. Melqart was an important Phoenician god and patron of the city of Tyre. He was especially worshipped at Tharson and Kition (see p. 36). As early as during the Cypro-Classical period, the representations of Herakles in Cypriote art and coins follow the classical Greek models. From the Hellenistic period, this way of representing of Herakles began to dominate. One of the most important Hellenistic statues representing Heracles was found in Golgoi-Hagios Photios (a site where a series of Heracles representations was found cf. Hermary and Mertens 2014, 226) and is now presented in the Musée du Louvre (cat. no. 112). The sculpture, dated to the end of the 4th century BC, follows the traditional representation of Greek Heracles. He is wearing a lion skin and raising his left arm to hold a club above his head. The expression on his face with mouth half-open with a faint smile and large eyes with deep corners follows a melancholy model characteristic for the beginning of Hellenistic sculpture. An interesting feature of Herakles' cult in Cyprus is the close connection there between the hero and Apollo. This is an aspect of Greek religious thought well-rooted in myth and underlined by local tradition. There are several Apollo sanctuaries in Cyprus where Herakles votives were found. This habit is especially well-documented in the sanctuary of Apollo Hylates in Kourion where, until the 1st century BC, some of the votive figurines dedicated to Apollo were made in moulds based on the Herakles type (Young and Young 1955).

Representations of Herakles continue well into Hellenistic and then Roman periods but his original importance as a counterpart of Apollo declined. It is difficult to point out any Herakles' statuette/statue dated to the Roman period found in a sanctuary or cultic context. The representations of Herakles are known mainly from little objects such as gems (Karageorghis 1998, 166) and olive lamps. For instance, from the 3rd century AD, local lamp makers copied a subject known from a Corinthian representation of Herakles fetching Kerberos

Figure 20. An olive lamp with representation of Herakles. Photo based on catalogue of Medelhavsmuseet Museum in Stockholm catalogue number 3913784.

from Hades. One example of this theme is preserved in the Medelhavsmuseet Museum in Stockholm (*Figure 20*). The statuary representations of Herakles are not rich. Among them, a statue from gymnasium of Salamis should be mentioned. It represents the so-called Farnese type with the torso leaning left toward an unpreserved support. This statue was found together with others in the east wing which were fully equipped during the reign of Trajan (Karageorghis 1969, 185). Others statuary representation of Heracles were found in the storage room of Villa of These in Nea Paphos. The barbed standing representation of a hero (dated to the 2nd century AD) could have been a part of a large group (Daszewski 1968, 53 pl.XI.5). Another statue (dated to the 4th century AD) represents the hero in a drunken state. Several Erotes surround him ready to steal his club. Finally, a small marble statue found in some debris next to the Salaminian theatre represents a young Herakles killing the snakes (Karageorghis 1998, 169). As most statues have been found in a secondary place with no inscriptions, no spatial analysis can be made. It seems, however, that all known representations had a mostly decorative significance. The Herakles myth was an inexhaustible source of inspiration. Recently (in July 2016) in Larnaca, a mosaic dated to the 2nd century AD was found. According to the first press news (cf. for example www.ekathimerini.com), that mosaic depicts the Labours of Herakles. Its discovery shows not only that ancient Kition, played a significant role in the establishment of Roman Cypriote culture but also underlines that Herakles remained a vivid element of that culture.

During the Hellenistic period in Cyprus, as in the other parts of empire, Herakles together with Hermes began to be worshipped as gods of the gymnasium. Dedications to both of them dated to the Roman period are known, for example, from gymnasium at Salamis. At Lapethos, at least during the period of Tiberius, there was a priest of gymnasium god. The formula hereus ton en gymnasioi theon could be identified with Hermes and Herakles. (Fujii 2013, 27-28). These connection between hero and the new, from the Cypriote point of view, sport, intellectual, and leisure institution—the gymnasium is particularly important to the religious image of Roman Cyprus. It indicates how polyvocal and flexible the image of the god-hero Herakles was.

Adonis

The myth of Adonis had an obviously Phoenician origin. He was consistently presented as an oriental divinity and the Phoenician city of Byblos was consecrated to him. It is possible that the cult of Adonis was introduced to Cyprus during the time when the Phoenicians had a strong influence on the island. The Adonis myth became one of the favorite themes among the Greek writers who connected the oriental god with Cyprian Aphrodite-Kypris (cf. Diogenianus, Corpus Paroemiographorum Graecorum I: 178, Clemens of Alexandria, Protrepticus: 2.29) In Greco-Roman mythology, Adonis was the son of Kinyras, king of Cyprus, who had been seduced by his daughter Myrrha (or Smyrna). Cursed by her father for seducing him, she fled to Syria where she was transformed into a myrrah tree, which then gave birth to a boy. Raised by nymphs, handsome young Adonis was taken by Aphrodite as her lover. However, Ares—the first lover of Aphrodite—soon discovered this affair. While Adonis was on a big game hunt the god of war transformed into a boar and killed the boy. Aphrodite searched for his body and found it in the sanctuary of Apollon Erithios in Cyprus (Photios, Bibliotheca: 190.152b). The mourning Aphrodite persuaded Zeus to permit Adonis to accompany Persephone during her half year on earth and half in the underworld. She also ordered a yearly festival in his memory.

The Cypriote version of the birth of Adonis from the incestuous love of Smyrna for her father Kinyras is present in the Greek texts from the Classical period. According to Photius (s.v. Adonios) allusions to Adonis were found in the comedies of Pherecrates, Plato, Cratinus, Aristophanes and others. The myth was also a subject of a play performed in the Roman times (Karageorghis 2005, 25). According to the myth, Adonis was the lover of the great goddess Aphrodite, so he was usually worshipped within her

Figure 21. An oinochoe from Amathous. Photo based on Hermary 2005, 48 fig. 6.

temenoi. In his text De dea Syria (6), Lucian described the adonai of Byblos as follows, '*I saw too at Byblos a large temple, sacred to the Byblian Aphrodite. This is the scene of the secret rites of Adonis*'. There was then a constant tendency to look for testimonies of the Adonis cult in the main Aphrodite sanctuaries in Cyprus. Pausanias (Hellados Periegesis: 9. 41. 2-3) quoted the story of a necklet preserved at Amathous in an old sanctuary consecrated to Aphrodite and Adonis. Also, Stephanus of Byzantium (Ethnica s.v. Amathous) defined Amathous as *a very ancient city of Cyprus where Adonis-Osiris, a god of Egyptian origin adopted by the Cypriotes and Phoenicians was venerated*. The excavations on the acropolis of Amathous have not brought to light any material connected to male cults. Still, we can link the hero and the city. Excavations of the cistern abutting the north wall of the city yielded a bronze oinochoe (*Figure 21*) with a dedication, Onesikrates son of Achaios made the offering to Helios Adonis in year 40, on the 7th of the month Romaios (Aupert 2008, 349-70). Although the association between Adonis and Helios was known from literary evidence (cf. Macrobius, Saturnalia: 1.21.11), this was the first archaeological material to provide proof. Adonis was a hero who after his death was shared between the world of death and the celestial domain of Helios—the Sun. The double name Helios Adonis underlines his dual nature and can be linked with rites of fertility so important in the religious landscape of Cyprus. According to Hermary (2015, 40), the mentioning of a specific date, the 7th of August in 9 or 18 AD (whether the chronological era begins in 31 or 22 BC) is not accidental and could be explained by a festival, perhaps Adonai, celebrated on that day. The finding from Amathous is not the only testimony of Adonis cult on the island.

Six kilometres from Palaipaphos functioned a sanctuary complex located on the hilltop of Lingrin tou Dhigeni in Rantidi Forest. The detailed study of pottery indicates the continued use of the site at least from the Cypro-Archaic and later through the late Roman period. During the archaeological works, many fragments of life-sized and over life-size terracotta statues were recovered, as well as more than 200 Cypro-syllabic inscriptions (Mitford and Masson, 1983). The detailed analyses of the material culture indicate that the sanctuary boasted an important cult of a male deity who was the consort of the goddess Aphrodite. A large natural cave found next to the site could be the location of oracular ceremonies (Bazermore 2002, 184). Moreover, as the area of temenos both contains and is surrounded by tombs, it is evident that the sacred space is strongly linked with connotations of death and resurrection. Unfortunately, none of the inscriptions known from the site are addressed to a patron of the sanctuary and only one of dubious interpretation (Mitford and Masson 1983, no. 1) points to a male deity. However, according to excavator of the site Georgina Bazemore, architectonic connotations are strong enough to support identification with Adonis. Another Cypriote city linked with Adonis is Idalion (*Plate 12*). According to the myth, ancient Idalion is a place where Adonis was killed by the jealous Ares. In 1992, the Expedition of University of Arizona team quite accidentally re-discovery the steps of the complex that for 120 years was labelled as 'Lang's Temple' (Gaber and Morden 1992, 21-30). The successive excavation works carried out in Mouti tou Arvili revealed an extensive outdoor sanctuary site founded in the late Geometric or early Archaic period. That temenos was in continuous use throughout the Roman period (Gaber and Dever 1996, 99-110; 2008, 48). From the very beginning, the sanctuary was dedicated to the Wanax—Lord. According to the director of Idalion excavations Pamela Gaber, Wanax in Cyprus very likely came to be called Adonis, perhaps in the Hellenistic period; certainly by the Roman era (Graber and Morden 1992; Gaber 1995; Gaber and Dever 1996, 48; Gaber 2008, 60) then the sanctuary of Mouti tou Arvili in Idalion appears to have been the sanctuary of Adonis. It must be underlined, however, that such a suggestion has not been unequivocally confirmed or widely accepted (cf. Tatton-Brown 2002, 245). Besides Amathous, Rantidi, and Idalion, the inscriptions and written sources tell us about at two other possible places where Adonis had a cult—Kition, and Salamis. It is also suggested that during the Roman period in Soloi-Cholades, the cult of Isis and Serapis may very possibly have coexisted with the cult of Aphrodite and Adonis since both Isis and Aphrodite lament the death of their beloved (Karageorghis 2005, 70).

Other possible heroic cults

Dioskouroi

There are very few references to the Dioskuroi in the cult related materials from Cyprus. According to Bennet (1980, 390), the function of these heroes was performed in Cyprus by others figures, including the Apollo and Herakles pair. It seems, however, that during the Roman period, the significance of heavenly twins increased. They are present in the list of testamentary gods of the Oath of loyalty to Tiberius, represented in sculptures from Soloi-Cholades and mentioned in a few inscriptions. Inter alia, a dedication from Salamis named the sons of Druzus Gaius and Lucius as the new Dioskuroi (Bennet 1980, 390). Probably the increase of significance of chthonic elements visible in Cypriote cults from the 1st century AD on the one hand, and the decrease in the significance of Herakles on the other, opened a space during the Roman period for certain motifs and archetypes connected with Dioskuroi.

Theseus and Ariadne

Citing Paion Amathousian writer, Plutarch in his Life of Theseus (20.2-4) described the local version of the myth of Ariadne. After leaving Crete, Theseus (*Plate 12*) and Ariadne were caught in a storm at sea. Theseus sent the pregnant and sick heroine to the shore while he tried to save his ship. However, the waves took him far off into the open sea. The native women of Amathous took care of Ariadne, trying to help her cope with her loneliness and when the abandoned heroine died in childbirth, she was buried on the island. Finally, Theseus came back, heard the whole sad story and decided to give some money to make a sacrifice to his beloved. The heroine received a tomb in a nearby sacred forest, two little statuettes were set up in her honour and a cult formed under the name of Ariadne-Aphrodite. A tomb hewn into the rock north of the Aphrodite temple and close to the acropolis cliff (cf. *Plate 2*) is frequently connected with this myth. A small path on the precise north-south orientation leads down to a narrow dromos and oval chamber. The most probable, based on its plan, the structure can be dated to the late Bronze Age/early Iron Age period. Nothing was found inside the tomb except some Cypro-Archaic sherds that cannot be associated with an inhumation, but rather with a religious ritual which post-dates the construction's phase. A large stone with a cluster of hollows found next to the dromos—an element popular in a Levantine necropolis—indicated the oriental connections of this tomb (Fourrier and Hermary 2006 16-21, 160-163). Its eminent position—the free-standing sepulchre structure on the top of hill, the remodelling works carried out at the beginning of the Archaic period when Amathousian sanctuary was developed, and the oriental connections—make it highly likely that the structure was related to the tomb of Ariadne-Aphrodite but proof is lacking (Aupert 2000, 71).

Still according to Paion's testimony, the second day of the month of Gorpaios was dedicated to the heroine. On that day, young men should lie in bed and mimic a woman's labour pains. This ceremony is also noted elsewhere in relation to a fertility cult. Unfortunately, no archaeological evidence confirms this practice.

Local deities

Opaon Melanthios

Twelve kilometers north of the Sanctuary of Aphrodite Paphia at Palaipaphos, in Amargetti, a sanctuary of a male rural deity is situated (Masson 1994). About twenty inscriptions have been discovered at the sanctuary which attest to the activity of the worship of the god known as Opaon Melanthios (Cayla 2018, 480-95 = I. Paphos nos. 312-336). Many interpretations for the meaning of the name Opaon Melanthios have been proposed. It is thought that his identity was conflated with the worship of Apollo and Pan. Epigraphic evidence support, at least in some cases, the identification with Apollo (Mitford 1946, 36-39; Masson 1983, 144). No doubt Opaon Melanthios exhibited the qualities of a traditional Cypriote Apollo. He was a rural deity who protected shepherds, huntsmen, and the inhabitants of the countryside. However, in contrast to Apollo who was a universal god, he was undoubtedly local in character. Numerous limestone representations of Opaon Melanthios have been found. Most of the representations fall into the realm of minor sculpture and follow simple iconographical models. He is depicted as a youthful man with a human face and the ears and horns of a faun. The statues stand on a plinth. The front of the god's body is always nude; the rest is occasionally covered by a heavy cloak. In one hand, he often holds a syrinx. Sometimes, perhaps under the influence of Priapos iconography, the god is represented ithyphallically (Karageorghis 1998, 192-193 - for Cypriote representations of Priapos see Karageorghis and Vermeule 1966, 21). According to Mitford (1946, 39), this cult may have outlived the Severian period.

It is significant that the monuments and offerings set up to this god at his sanctuary were done so by men only, which stands in great contrast to the inscriptions discovered at the sanctuary of Aphrodite Paphia. The appearance of two inscriptions set up by a quaestor provinciae, at this rural sanctuary, to the heirs of Augustus is significant and shows the importance of local cults within the sacred landscape of Cyprus. Beside the Amargetti sanctuary, statuettes of the god Pan/Opaon Melanthios have been discovered across the island in Lefkoniko, the temple of Aphrodite in Golgoi and in the sanctuary of Apollo at Vouni (Flourentzos 1989, Karageorghis 2000, 261).

Theos Hypsistos

The existence of Theo Hypsistos, or sometimes Theos Hypsistos, in the religious landscape of the Mediterranean region has been demonstrated from the Hellenistic period to the 5th century AD. Various studies have shown that although Hypsistos was used by the Jews to denote Yahve (Trebilco 1991, 129-131), the appearance of Hypsistos across the Roman Empire does not explicitly signal the practice or influence of Judaism. The name of Hypsistos was also used by non-Jews to designate the other god—Zeus. Paul Trebilco's study (1991, particularly chapter six) of the use of this epithet in Asia Minor demonstrates that the name in fact could be used by an individual to denote the god whom he personally viewed as the most important. It must be underlined that the cult is not limited to the poleis only, and monuments with his name are known from the Roman chora. Many of the inscriptions invoking Theos Hypsistos were prayers for good harvests and dedications from those suffering from illnesses (Mitchell 1999, 125).

In Cyprus, the worship of Theos Hypsistos has been epigraphically demonstrated mainly in area of Limassol (e.g. in Amathous, Agios Athanasios, Polemidhia) and Paphos region both in Nea Paphos polis and in the Palaipaphos sanctuary. The epigraphic evidence for the worship of Theos Hypsistos was not exclusive to these two regions—inscriptions dedicated to the god have been also discovered at Kourion, and Kition (Mitchell 1999, 144-145). His marble statue is known from Kourion (*Figure 22*). According to epigraphical testimony, another statue of Hypnos was dedicated in Salamis to Aphrodite Oreia. Bennet (1980, 435) noted that the connection between the Hypnos and Aphrodite Oreia identified as Kybele may have something to do with their role in medicine. In this context, a group of four inscriptions found in the 1890's at Golgoi is extremely interesting. The dedications to Hypsistos were part of anatomical ex vota in the form of flat plaques with suspensions holes. On three plaques, the features are traced by an incision and the inscription is painted. These plaques were dedicated by men. A fourth ex-voto with a pair of breasts in relief was dedicated by a woman. So far the anatomical ex vota in Cyprus, as those found at Golgoi, were found only within the inland sanctuaries in a rural context. The reason for this is obscure. The form in which the name of Theos Hypnos is mentioned in all plaques points that he was treated as a local healing god (Michaelides 2014, 31-32).

Figure 22. Marble torso of Theos Hypnos from Kourion. Episcopi museum. Photo by the author.

TOWARDS MONOTHEISM

Jews, most probably, were settled in Cyprus from the time of Ptolemy Philadelphus, who reigned between 309-246 BC (Hill 1940, 241). Despite the limited material evidence for the presence of Jews in Cyprus during the Hellenistic period, Josephus Flavius underlined (Antiquitates Iudaicae, 13.284) that there was a flourishing Jewish community in his times. According to Talmud (Yoma: IV.5; cf. Kapera 2009, 33), the Cypriote Jews were obliged to supply wine for the Jerusalem temple. Many of them lived in Salamis. When St Barnabas and Paul landed at Cyprus they proclaimed the word of God in that city in the synagogues of the Jews (Acts of the Apostles: 13.5). Salamis was destroyed during empire-wide Jewish revolt in AD 115/6. Cassius Dio (68.32.1-3 cf. also Eusebius, Historiae Ecclesiastica: 4.2) noted that as many as 240,000 Cypriots died during this conflict. Trajan sent the Legio VII Claudia to Cyprus to quash the revolt and when it restored peace, the Jews were moved out of Cyprus and thereafter not allowed to set foot on it under pain of death. Although this anecdote is thought to be greatly exaggerated, still the total absence of Jewish symbols in Cyprus, more particularly in the funerary context, is worth mentioning (cf. Mitford 1990, 2205). As both epigraphical and archaeological data are scarce, it is difficult to gain a full insight into the Jewish communities of Roman Cyprus. Equally little is known about the emerging Christian community—we cannot point to where they resided, their identity and experience of Romanity. The data that we have indicates a rather peaceful and gradual development. Quite early on, church structures were raised near the major Cypriote sanctuaries, also those mentioned by Tacitus, with both Paphos and Salamis represented by bishops at Council of Ephesus in 324. Unfortunately, evidence of the early Christian cult is extremely fragmentary and falls outside the framework of this study.

CONCLUSIONS

From the Hellenistic period, the sacred landscape of Cyprus began to be significantly remodelled.

It seems that in the process of building a pan-Cypriote cultural identity, the number of cultic places was noticeably reduced. It was repeatedly demonstrated that many Iron-Age Cyprus sanctuaries signalled frontiers between adjacent political units. Besides helping to define kingdom boundaries, they also represented the ruling elite's attempts to establish a sense of territorial identity and loyalty among the local inhabitants (Rupp 2000, 1098). After the period of city-kingdoms with extra-urban sanctuaries connected to their boundaries, Cyprus was ruled as one organism from the Hellenistic period. In line with the political circumstances, there was a change in the religious landscape. Boundary sanctuaries as 'official' cult places lost their significance. If they were not abandoned, they changed their status and became rural—primarily used by locals and insignificant for the wider community. This process did not stop with the end of the Ptolemaic era. Many inland sanctuaries, like the sanctuary of Pair Deities in Idalion, were active until the 1st century AD only.

It must be underlined, however, that very often the available material originates from research conducted in the 19th century when little attention was focused on stratigraphic sequences. As most of votary gifts are dated on a stylistic basis, the chronological span of Cypriotes sanctuaries can only be roughly analysed. Sometimes the sanctuary was in use much longer than previously believed. The recent excavation work still conducted in Idalion demonstrated that another sanctuary dedicated to Adonis not only was still active until the middle Roman period but also much of the rebuilding work was carried out during this time. Also, detailed research made in the region of Mesoaria Plain (Athienou Archaeological Project) indicates that there was no sudden decrease in cultic activity. Another important fact is that the process of reducing the number of active sanctuaries did not reflect any change in the settlement's patterns. Although it is true that the Paphos region was depopulated, as confirmed by both archaeological works and literary evidence, that process did not encompass the whole island. Parks (1999, 119), who analysed burial and settlement patterns in Hellenistic and Roman Cyprus, suggested that the study of funerary landscapes indicated a much more extensive settlement system for the inland regions of the island than had previously been believed. Also new research conducted by Vasiliki Lysandrou and Athos Agapiou (2015) confirms that most of the necropoleis from the Hellenistic period were still in use during Roman times. Moreover, according to the data they collected, several necropoleis, including those located inland (including the mountainous region of Limassol District), were primarily and entirely Roman. The reduced number of sanctuaries seems to follow the major change in settlement patterns which, according to Rautman (2000, 317), began to decline around the 2nd century AD.

The continuity and discontinuity of the inland sanctuaries should not be attributed to mechanisms of social memory and political needs. The cultic activity was centred primary around the coastal cities. It seems that none of the inland sanctuaries were rebuilt under the imperial patronage. There were four main sanctuaries that developed significantly during Roman period: Soloi-Cholades in the north, Salamis in the east, Palaiopaphos, Kourion, and Amathous in the south. The domination of the southern part of the island is not a coincidence. It reflects the organization of the trading system and, therefore, the interest of the Roman administration. The architecture of Soloi-Cholades and Palaiopaphos followed the traditional model of a Cypriote sanctuary based on oriental architecture with a large court and little cultic building defined as a prime unit in itself situated in natural surroundings and more or less independent of any urban development (Wright 1992, 188). Although the Soloi-Cholades site was developed in the Ptolemaic and Roman period only, it consists of large square courts that communicated with small rooms that formed the holy-of-holies. With the passage of time, the buildings increased in number and became more monumental but never acquired the form of a Greek-style temple. The same pattern is visible in the sanctuary of Aphrodite in Palaipaphos. As a domicile of koinon Kyprion and pan-Mediterranean pilgrimage centre, the sanctuary both for locals and roman administration played the most important role in social communication. As such, it was significant expanded. Many additional structures were built but the sacred spacial arrangement remained close to the traditional Cypriot temenos. Also, the cult statue of the goddess retained the archaic aniconic shape of the baetyl (Wright 1992, 188). The description of the tripartire Palaipaphos sanctuary on the Roman coins issued by the koinon Kyprion underlines the significance of these 'Cypriote' religious traditions up to the late imperial period.

The Greek temple model was introduced to the architecture of the sanctuaries of Apollo Hylates in Kourion, Aphrodite in Amathous acropolis, and Zeus Olympiaios in Salamis, perhaps during the late Hellenistic period. However, as K. Butcher demonstrates (2010), the appearance of such a temple should not be considered as a rupture from past tradition. Indeed, beside the change in appearance of the temple and the significant phase of rebuilding done during early Roman period, the change in the internal space arrangement of the sanctuaries seems to have been minimal. Unfortunately, we do not know much about the main Salaminian sanctuary which is still mostly unearthed. Both in the sanctuary of Aphrodite in Amathous and Apollo Hylates in Kourion the places of importance for religious proposes—elements such as archaic altars, Round Building in Kourion, so-called Ariadne tomb in Amathous remained unchanged.

The uninterrupted development can be observed not only in the sacred landscape but also in religious practice. The god patrons of the main sanctuaries remained the same: Aphrodite in Amathous and Palaipaphos; Zeus Olympius in Salamis. Soloi-Cholades continued the cult of Aphrodite, Isis, while in Kourion the patron god was Apollo Hylates.

As in previous periods, the most important element of Cyprote beliefs was Aphrodite Kypris. Her rank differed much from a conventional image of the goddess of love and beauty. She was an ancient powerful divinity and her cult was based on fertility rituals that were very important for Cypriote religious practice. The cult of Aphrodite flourished first of all in the Palaipaphos sanctuary that, under the protection of the Roman emperors, became a pan-Mediterranean pilgrimage centre. It seems that cult practices in other Cypriote sanctuaries of Aphrodite were of minor importance. Even the old and prestigious sanctuary in Amathousian Acropolis seems to not have been very active and as archaeological material indicates could have been abandoned as early as the 3rd century AD.

The history of Apollo was somehow parallel to that of Aphrodite. Although the iconography of votives and cult statues depicting the god following mainly (but not exclusively) Greek models, many elements of cultic practice were more rooted in the local tradition. The close relation of god with the nature and animals is especially visible. In the main Apollo sanctuary in Kourion, as well as in Nea Paphos, he is venerated under the local epithet—Hylates. There were also several Apollo sanctuaries in the Mesoaria plain and most of them had a rural feel. The standard ex vota found there depicted Apollo with a wreath of plants that possess medicinal attributes. This kind of offerings were certainly involved in some rituals held for the regeneration of the agriculture cycle.

Without any doubt, Aphrodite and Apollo played a major role in the religious landscape of Cyprus. Due to the state of the archaeological works in Salamis the rank of the main god of the city—Zeus is not well recognised and other Olympian gods although visible especially in epigraphical testimonies were of the minor importance. It seems that Cypriote beliefs were mainly focused on the fertility powers of the deity.

Therefore, it is not surprising that the local cults of local gods were still visible in the Roman period. The best example is the cult of Opaon Melanthios in the sanctuary located in Armagetti. The appearance of two inscriptions set up by a quaestor provinciae to the heirs of Augustus is significant and shows the importance of local cults within the sacred landscape of Cyprus.

At first glance, it seems that apart from the gods, the heroes were an important element of Cypriote beliefs. There is an abundant mythological material concerning the founder heroes of Cypriote cities. From literary evidence, the hero cult of historical Onesilis and Kimon is also known. Unfortunately, the archaeological material does not indicate any specific cultic practice connected with them. In Paphos and Salamis, the foundation myths were used by local kings to strengthen their political power. From the Ptolemiac period, their importance for local identify mostly declined. Only in the Roman period do the inscriptions from Kourion underline the close connection between the polis and its founder Perseus. It seems that among the demigods related to Cyprus, only the presence of Herakles and Adonis is well demonstrated in religious-related material. However, neither of them was a classical Greek hero. Adonis, an oriental god and patron of Byblos, in the Greek myths was a son of Kyrinas and the beloved of Aphrodite. As his story is strongly linked with Cyprus there is a frequent tendency to look for elements that fit Adonis in cultic-related material. He was proposed as a patron deity of two sanctuaries, one in Idalion and another in Rantidi. However, up to now only a bronze oinochoe found in the cistern in Amathous confirmed his cult.

The roots of the worship of Herakles in Cyprus are obscure. Many of the local cults are probably Hellenised versions of practices dedicated to Phoenician Melqart. An interesting feature of Herakles' cult in Cyprus is the close connection there between the hero and Apollo. There are several Apollo sanctuaries in Cyprus where votary representations of

Herakles were found. Representations of Herakles continue well into Hellenistic and then Roman periods but his original importance as a counterpart of Apollo decreased. The images of the hero are visible in a domestic context. He is depicted on objects of everyday use such as olive lamps and on mosaic representations. We know also of the statuary representations, but it is difficult to point to any dated to Roman period Herakles' statuette/statue found in a sanctuary or in a cultic context. As a heroic cult was not an important element of Cypriote religious practice before, neither during the Roman period did the worship of heroes did occur with the same intensity as in the others parts of the Empire. It is true that many mythic stories are set on the island and the literary material about the heroic cult also during the Roman period is fascinating, but all the accounts that we have were written from the position of an outside observer. They tell us more about romanitas than about the local identity. Looking on the frustrating lack of its evidence in archaeological material, it seems that although consistently present in ancient literature, the cult of heroes was not a part of Cypriote religion tradition.

Somehow in the opposition to the cult of heroes, the cult of roman emperors is visible. As in the other eastern provinces, the cult of the emperor was introduced to the sanctuaries of traditional deities. Two inscriptions from Amathous attest to a sanctuary of Aphrodite and Titus. There was also a cult of Apollo Hylates and Apollo Caesar in Kourion and perhaps a cult of Zeus Caesar in Salamis. Both cultic and honorific statues of imperial family members were placed within Cypriote temenoi and set in the public space, in theatres and gymnasia. The constant presence of the emperor in the religious landscape was also strengthened by numerous festivals that were introduced to the Cypriote calendar.

The tradition of the open sanctuary, the strong cult of Aphrodite as a fertility goddess, the cult of Apollo, the minor importance of the worship of heroes on the one side and the centralization of the cult in costal sanctuaries, introducing the Greek temple model and the cult of the ruler on the other—all of this evidence taken together provides a complex image of the religion of Cyprus combining the oldest cult traditions with new pan-Mediterranean ones.

Of course, during the whole Roman period, religion did not remain consistently the same. The patterns of worship, as they are very fragile to people's needs and hopes, are in an incessant change. In Cyprus, like in others part of the Mediterranean, after the 1st century AD, chthonic elements started to be more visible. Surprisingly enough, the evidence of mysterious practices is really scarce. Due to architectural similarities, the Temple F in Soloi-Cholades and Underground Sanctuary in Garrison Camp are sometimes indicated as Mithrea but nothing more supports this interpretation.

Very interesting are the testimonies against the cult of Theos Hypnos. Although Hypsistos was used by the Jews to denote Yahve, the appearance of the gods across the Roman Empire does not explicitly signal the practice or influence of Judaism. Bennet (1980, 435) noted that in Cyprus, there was a connection between the Hypnos and Aphrodite Oreia that may have something to do with their role in medicine. The anatomical ex vota from Golgoi with dedications to Theos Hypnos confirms that he was perceived as a local healing god.

Unfortunately, we do not know much about religious practices after the Severian dynasty. The lack of epigraphical testimonies hinders research on Cypriote religion. It seems that the process of the decline in cultic activity advanced if not accelerated. However, other places, including inland ones like the sanctuary of Zeus Labrianos in Phasoula, demonstrate the unbelievable continuity of cult practice until the late 4th century AD. The late Roman history of the Cypriote religion is yet to be written.

REFERENCES

Amandry, M.
2016   Cypriote coinage under Roman rule (30 BC – 3rd century AD) kyprioscharacter.eie.gr/en/t/AT (Accessed: 01/05/2016).

Anastassiades, A.
1998   Ἀρσινόης Φιλαδέλφου: Aspects of a specific cult in Cyprus, RDAC 1998: 129-40.
2003   Fusion and Diffusion. Isiac Cults in Ptolemaics and Roman Cyprus in: D. Michaelides, V. Kassianidou, and R. S. Merrillees (eds.), Egypt and Cyprus in Antiquity, Oxford, 144-50.

Argoud, G. et al.
1975   G. Argoud, O. Callot, B. Helly, A-M. Larribeau, Le temple de Zeus à Salamine, RDAC 1975: 122-41.

Aupert, P.
1996   Guide, Sites et Monuments XV, Paris.
2000   Guide to Amathus, Nicosia.
2008   Hélios, Adonis et magie: les trésors d'une citerne d'Amathonte (Inscriptions d'Amathonte VIII), BCH 132.2: 347-87.
2009   Amathonte hellénistique et romaine: l'apport des travaux récents, CCEC 39: 25-48.

Aupert, P. and Hermary, A.
1981   Rapport sur les travaux de l'École française à Amathonte en 1975, BCH 105.2: 1025-34.
2006   Nouveaux documents sur le culte d'Aphrodite à Amathonte, BCH 130.1: 83-115.

Aupert, P. and Masson, O.
1979   Inscriptions d'Amathonte I, BCH 103.1: 361-89.

Bagnall, R. S. and Drew-Bear, T.
1973   Documents from Kourion: A Review Article Part 2: Individual Inscriptions', Phoenix 27.3: 213-44.

Baurain, C.
1980   Kinyras: la fin de l'âge du bronze à Chypre et la tradition antique, BCH 104.2: 277-308.

Bazermore, G.B.
2002   The display and viewing of the syllabic inscriptions of Rantidi Sanctuary, in: J. S. Smith (ed.), Script and Seal Use on Cyprus in the Bronze and Iron Ages, Boston, 155-212.

Bennett, C.G.
1980 The Cults of the ancient Greek Cypriotes, PhD dissertation.

Bicknell, P. J.
1977 Caesar, Antony, Cleopatra and Cyprus, Latomus 36: 325-42.

Bekker-Nielsen, T.
2004 The Roads of Ancient Cyprus, Copenhagen.

Butcher, K.
2010 Contesting sacred space in Lebanese temples in: E. S. Gruen (ed.), Cultural identity in the ancient Mediterranean. Issues & debates, Los Angeles, 452-63.

Buitron, D. and Soren, D.
1980 Missouri in Cyprus: The Kourion Expedition, Muse 13: 22-31.

Cassimatis, H.
1982 À propos de couronnes surles têtes masculines en calcaire de Chypre, RDAC 1982: 156-63.

Cayla, J.-B.
2001 À propos de Kinyras: Nouvelle lecture d'une épiclèse d'Apollon à Chypre, CCEC 31: 69-81.
2004 Livie, Aphrodite et une famille de prêtres du culte impériale à Paphos in: S. Follet (ed.), L'hellénisme d'époque romaine: nouveaux documents, nouvelles approches (Ier s.a.C. -IIIe s.p.C.), Paris, 233-43.
2018 Les inscriptions de Paphos. La cité chypriote sous la domination lagide et à l'époque impériale, Lyon.

Cesnola, A. P. di
1882 Salaminia (Cyprus): the history, treasures, & antiquities of Salamis in the island of Cyprus, London.

Cesnola, L. P. di
1877 Cyprus: Its Ancient Cities, Tombs and Temples, London.

Christou, D.
1996 Kourion. Its Monuments and Local Museum, Nicosia.

Counts, D.
2009 From Siwa to Cyprus: The Assimilation of Zeus Ammon in the Cypriote Pantheon in: D. Michaelides, V. Kassianidou, and R. Merrillees (eds.), Egypt and Cyprus in Antiquity, Oxford, 104-17.

Counts, D. and Toumazou, M. K.
2003 Artemis at Athienou-Malloura, CCEC 33: 237-51.

Daszewski, W. A.
1968 A Preliminary Report on the Excavations of the Polish Archaeological Mission at Kato (Nea) Paphos in 1966 and 1967, RDAC 1968: 33-61.

Flourentzos, P.
1989 The Iconography of the God Pan in Cypriot Sculpture, RDAC 1989: 121-26.
2007 An unknown Graeco-Roman temple from the lower town of Amathous, CCEC 37: 299-306.

Fortin, M.
1980 Fondation de Villes Grecques à Chypre: Légendes et Découvertes Archéologiques in: J.B. Caron, M. Fortin and G. Maloney (eds.), Mélanges D'études Anciennes offerts à Maurice Lebel, Québec, 25-44.
1984 Nouvelles découvertes relatives aùx légendes de fondation de villes Grecques à Chypre à la fin de l'âge du bronze, Echos du Monde Classique/Classical Views 3: 133-46.

Fourrier, S.
2008 Légendes de fondation et hellénisation de Chypre. Parcours historiographique, CCEC 38:103-118

Fourrier, S. and Hermary, A.
2006 Amathonte VI: le sanctuaire d'Aphrodite des origines au début de l'époque impériale, Paris.

Franklin, J.C.
2015 Kinyras: The Divine Lyre, Cambridge and London.

Fujii, T.
2013 Imperial Cult, Imperial Representation in Roman Cyprus, Stuttgart.
2015 Imperial Cult and Imperial Statues in Roman Cyprus: A Preliminary Report in: A. Jacobs and P. Cosyns (eds.), Cypriot Material Culture Studies from Picrolite Carving to Proskynitaria Analysis. Proceedings of the 8th Annual Postgraduate Cypriot Archaeology Conference Held in Honour of the Memory of Paul Åström at the Vrije Universiteit Brussel (Belgium), 27th - 29th November 2008, Brussels, 245-56.

Gaber, P.
1995 The History of Ancient Idalion in the Light of Recent Excavations in: P.W. Wallace (ed.), Visitors, Immigrants and Invaders in Cyprus, Suny, 32-39.
2008 The History of History: Excavations at Idalion and the Changing History of a City Kingdom, Near Eastern Archaeology 71.1-2: 52-63.

Gaber, P. and Dever, W.G
1996 Idalion, Cyprus: Conquest and Continuity in: W.G. Dever (ed.), Preliminary Excavation Reports, Sardis, Idalion, and Tell El-Handaquq North, AASOR 53: 85-113.

Gaber, P. and Morden, M.
1992 University of Arizona Expedition to Idalion, CCEC 18: 21-26.

Given, M. and Knapp, A.B. (eds.)
2003 The Sydney Cyprus Survey Project: Social Approaches to Regional Archaeological Survey, Los Angeles.

Gjerstad, E.
1944 The Colonization of Cyprus in Greek Legend, OpArch 3: 107-23.

Gordon J.M.
2012 Between Alexandria and Rome: A Postcolonial Archaeology of Cultural Identity in Hellenistic and Roman Cyprus, PhD Dissertation.

Graf, F.
2009 Apollo, London-New York.

Guidice et al.
2017 F. Giudice, E. Giudice, G. Guidice and S.C. Chiarello, Paphos, Garrison's camp. XIIa campagna (1999), AnnRepCypr 2011-12: 771-809.

Hayes, J.W.
1967 Cypriot Sigillata, RDAC 1967: 65-77.
1977 Early Roman Wares from the House of Dionysos, Paphos, Rei Cretariae Romanae Fautorum acta 17/18: 96-108.

Hedreen, G.
1991 The Cult of Achilles in the Euxine, Hesperia 60: 13-31.

Hermary, A.
1990 Cinq ex-voto d'Arsos retrouvés au Musée du Louvre, CCEC 14: 45-48.
1992 Le sanctuaire de Zeus Labranios a Phasoula in: G.C. Ioannides (ed.), Studies in honour of Vassos Karageorghis, Nicosia, 333-37.
1994 La Date du Temple D' Aphrodite À Amathonte, BCH 118: 321-30.
2009 Un Apollon Chypriote aux boucles 'Lybiques in: D. Michaelides, V. Kassianidou, R. S. Merrillees (eds.), Egypt and Cyprus in Antiquity, Oxford, 136-143.
2015 Amathus, capital of the Kingdom and city-state in: A. Nicolaou Konnari and C. Schabel (eds.), Lemesos: A History of Limassol in Cyprus from Antiquity to the Ottoman Conquest, Cambrigde, 1-49.

Hermary, A. and Mertens, J.
2014 The Cesnola Collection of Cypriot Art: Stone Sculpture, Yale.

Hill, G.F.
1940   A History of Cyprus. Volume 1 To the Conquest by Richard the Lion Heart, Cambridge.

Hogarth, D.G. et al.
1888   Hogarth, D.G., James, M.R., Elsey Smith, R. and Gardner, E.A., Excavations in Cyprus, 1887-88. Paphos, Leontari, Amargetti, JHS 9: 147-271.

Hunt, A.
2016   Reviving Roman Religion: Sacred Trees in the Roman World, Cambridge.

Hussein, E.
2014   Power and identity in Roman Cyprus, Ph.D Dissertation.

Ioannou, Ch.
2015   http://kyprioscharacter.eie.gr/en/scientific-texts/details/cyprus-and-others/cypriotes-and-phoenicians (Accessed: 01/05/2016).

Kantiréa, M.
2008   Le culte impérial à Chypre: relecture des documents épigraphiques, ZPE 167: 91-112.
2010   Apollon Hylatès et Apollon César à Kourion: Contribution épigraphique à la topographique du sanctuaire, CCEC 40: 253-75.

Kapera, Z.J.
2009   The Jewish Presence in Cyprus before AD 70, Scripta Judaica Cracoviensia 7: 33-44.

Karageorghis, J.
2005   Kypris. The Aphrodite of Cyprus. Ancient Sources and Archaeological Evidence, Nicosia.

Karageorghis, V.
1969   Salamis in Cyprus: Homeric, Hellenistic and Roman, London.
1998   Greek Gods and Heroes in Ancient Cyprus, Athens.
2000   Ancient Art from Cyprus: The Cesnola Collection in the Metropolitan Museum of Art, New York.

Karageorghis, V. and Vermeule, C.C.
1964   Sculptures from Salamis. Vol. 1, Nicosia.
1966   Sculptures from Salamis. Vol. 2, Nicosia.

Kleibl, K.
2007   Der hellenistisch-römisch Temple gräco-ägyptischer Götter in Soli in: S. Rogge (ed.), Materielle Kulturen auf Zypern bis in die römische Zeit, Münster, 125-50.

Lavelle, B.M.
1984   Herodotos on the Argives of Kourion, Hermes 112.2: 249-52.

Leonard, J.R.
1995   Evidence for Roman Ports, Harbours and Anchorages in Cyprus in: V. Karageorghis and D. Michaelides (eds.), Cyprus and the Sea, Nicosia, 227-42.

Lysandrou, V. and Agapiou, A.
2015   Cities of the dead: approaching the lost landscape of Hellenistic and Roman necropoleis of Cyprus, Archaeological and Anthropological Sciences 8.4: 867-77.

Maier, F.G.
1975   The Temple of Aphrodite at Old Paphos, RDAC 1975: 69-80.

Maier, F.G. and Karageorghis, V.
1984   Paphos: History and Archaeology, Nicosia.

Manning, S. et al.
2002   S. Manning, A. Manning, R. Tomber, D.A. Sewell, S.J. Monsks, M.J. Ponting and E.C. Ribeiro, The Late Roman Church at Maroni Petrera: Survey and Salvage Excavations 1990-1997, and Other Traces of Roman Remains in the Lower Maroni Valley, Cyprus, Nicosia.

Masson, O.
1980   Notes sur un sanctuaire d'Arsos, BCH 104.1: 273-75.
1983   Les Inscriptiones Chypriotes Syllabiques, Paris.
1994   Amargetti, un sanctuaire rural près de Paphos, BCH 118.1: 261-75.

Michaelides, D.
1990   The Roman Period. 30 BC - AD 330 in: D. Hunt (ed.), Footprints in Cyprus, London, 110-35.
1996   The Economy of Cyprus during the Hellenistic and Roman periods in: V. Karageorghis and D. Michaelides (eds.), The Development of the Cypriot Economy: From the prehistoric period to the present day, Nicosia, 139-52.
2009   A boat-shaped lamp from Nea Paphos and the divine protectors of navigation in CCEC 39: 197-226.
2014   The anatomical ex-votos of Hellenistic and Roman Cyprus in: D. Michaelides (ed.), Medicine and Healing in the Ancient Mediterranean, Oxford, 30-37.

Michaelidou-Nicolaou, I.
1978   The cult of Oriental Divinities in Cyprus: Archaic to Graeco-Roman Times in: M. de Boer and T. A. Edridge (eds.), Hommages à Maarten J. Vermaseren, Volume 2, Leiden, 791-800.

Mitchell, S.
1999   The cult of theos hypsistos between pagans, Jews, and Christians, in: P. Athanassiadi and M. Frede (eds.), Pagan Monotheism in Late Antiquity, Oxford, 81-149.

Mitford, T.B.
1946   Religious documents from Roman Cyprus, JHS 66: 24-42.

1947 Notes on some published Inscriptions from Roman Cyprus, BSA 42: 201-30.
1950 New Inscriptions from Roman Cyprus, OpArch 6: 1-95.
1957 Ptolemy Macron in: E. Arslan (ed.), Studi in onore di Aristide Calderini e Roberto Paribeni. Vol. 2 Studi di papirologia e antichità orientale, Milano, 163-87.
1960 A Cypriot Oath of Allegiance to Tiberius, JRS 50: 75-9.
1961a The Hellenistic Inscriptions of Old Paphos, BSA 56: 1-41.
1961b Further contributions to the epigraphy of Cyprus, AJA 65: 93-151.
1971 The Inscriptions of Kourion, Philadelphia.
1980 Roman Cyprus, Aufstieg und Niedergang der römischen Welt II. 7.2: 1285-384.
1990 The Cults of Roman Cyprus, Aufstieg und Niedergang der römischen Welt II 18.3: 2176-211.

Mitford, T.B. and Masson, O.
1983 The Syllabic Inscriptions of Rantidi-Paphos, Costance.

Młynarczyk, J.
1980 The Paphian Sanctuary of Apollo Hylates, RDAC 1980: 239-52.
1990 Nea Paphos in the Hellenistic period, Warszawa.

Moore, R.S.
2003 Hellenistic to Roman Landscapes in: M. Given and A.B. Knapp (eds.), Social Approaches to Regional Archaeological Survey: The Sydney Cyprus Survey Project, Los Angeles.

Nicolaou, I.
1976 The Historical Topography of Kition, SIMA 43, Göteborg.

Oppen de Ruiter, B.F. van
2007 Religious Identification of Ptolemaic Queens with Aphrodite, Demeter, Hathor and Isis, New York.

Papageorghiou, A.
1985 L'architecture paleochretienne de Chypre, Corso di cultura sull'arte ravennate e byzantina 32: 299-324.

Papantoniou, G.
2009 "Revisiting" Soloi-Cholades: Ptolemaic Power, Religion and Ideology, CCEC 39: 271-87.
2012 Religion and Social Transformations in Cyprus. From the Cypriot Basileis to the Hellenistic Strategos, Leiden- Boston.
2015 From the Cypriot Basileis to the Hellenistic Strategos: The Archaeological Evidence http://kyprioscharacter.eie.gr/en/scientific-texts/details/kingdoms-kings/fromcypriot-basileis-to-hellenistic-strategos-archaeological-evidence (Accessed: 01/07/2016).

Papantoniou, G. and Vionis, A.K.
2017 Landscape Archaeology and Sacred Space in the Eastern Mediterranean: A Glimpse from Cyprus, Land 6.40: 1-18.

Parks, D.A.
1999 Burial customs of Roman Cyprus: origin and development. PhD Dissertation.

Petrie, W.M.F.
1927 Objects of daily use, London.

Pfeiffer, S.
2008 The god Serapis, his cult and the beginnings of the ruler cult in Ptolemaic Egypt in: P. McKechnie, and P. Guillame (eds.), Ptolemy II Philadelphus and his world, Leiden-Boston, 387-408.

Pirenne-Delforge, V.
1994 L'Aphrodite grecque, Kernos Supplément IV, Athènes-Liège.

Potter, D.
2000 Ἡ Κύπρος ἐπαρχία τῆς Ρωμαϊκῆς Αὐτοκρατορίας in: T. Papadopoullos (ed.), Ἱστορία τῆς Κύπρου Vol. 2, Ἀρχαία Κύπρος, Part 2, Nicosia, 763-864.

Price, S.R.F.
1984 Gods and Emperors: The Greek Language of the Roman Imperial Cult, JHS 104: 79-95.

Rautman, M.
2000 The busy countryside of Late Roman Cyprus, RDAC 2000: 317-31.

Raptou, E.
1996 Contribution to the study of the economy of ancient Cyprus: copper-timber in: V. Karageorghis and D. Michaelides (eds.), The development of the Cypriot economy from the prehistoric period to the present day, Nicosia, 249-59.

Rowe, A.H.
2004 Reconsidering Late Roman Cyprus: Using new material from Nea Paphos to review current artefact typologies, PhD Dissertation.

Rupp, D.
2000 Map 72 Cyprus in: R.J.A. Talbert (ed.), Barrington Atlas of the Greek and Roman World: Map-by-map, Princeton-Oxford, 1085-107.

Scranton, R.
1967 The Architecture of the Sanctuary of Apollo Hylates at Kourion, Transactions of the American Philosophical Society: New Series 57.5: 3-85.

Sinos, S.
1990 The Temple of Apollo Hylates at Kourion and the Restoration of Its SouthWest Corner, Athens.

Solomidou- Ieronymidou, M.
1985 The ancient religion of Cyprus through the epigraphical documents of Cyprus and Greece: a comparative study, Archaeologia Cypria 1: 57-64.

Soren, D.
1987 The Excavation and its Significance in: D. Soren (ed.), The Sanctuary of Apollo Hylates at Kourion, Cyprus, Tuscon, 24-52.

Tatton-Brown, V.
2002 The kingdom of Idalion. Lang's excavations in the British Museum, CCEC 32: 243-56.

Teixidor, J.
1983 L'interprétation phénicienne d'Héraclès et d'Apollon, Revue de l'histoire des religions 200: 243-45.

Trebilco, P.R.
1991 Jewish communities in Asia Minor, Cambridge.

Ulbrich, A.
2008 Kypris: Heiligtümer und Kulte weiblicher Gottheiten auf Zypern in der Kyproarchaischen und Kyproklassischen Epoche (Königszeit), Münster.
2010 Images of Cypriot Aphrodite in her Sanctuaries during the Age of the City-Kingdoms in: A.C. Smith and S. Pickup (eds.), Brill's Companion to Aphrodite. Leiden - Boston, 167-93.

Vermeule, C.C.
1976 Greek and Roman Cyprus: Art from Classical through Late Antique Times, Boston.

Vernet, Y.
2011 L'Apollon chypriote, de la nature et des animaux, CCEC 41: 251-64.
2015 The Cypriote Apollo. Characteristics of the Apolline Cult in Cyprus, http://kyprioscharacter.eie.gr/en/scientific-texts/details/cult-and-religion/cypriote-apollo-characteristics-of-apolline-cult-in-cyprus (Accessed: 01/07/2016).

Veymiers, R.
2005 Sérapis face au sanctuaire Paphia. À propos d'une gemme disparue de la collection Petrie in: Chr. Cannuyer (ed.), La langue dans tous ses états. Michel Malaise in honorem, Louvain, 339-56.

Voros, G.
2007 Field Research IX: Nea Paphos in: G. Voros (ed.), Egyptian Temple Architecture: 100 years of Hungarian Excavations in Egypt, 1907-2007, Budapest, 117-202.

Westholm, A.
1936 The temples of Soli: studies on Cypriote art during Hellenistic and Roman periods, Stockholm.

Wilburn, A.T.
2005 Materia magica: the archaeology of magic in Roman Egypt, Cyprus and Spain, Ann Arbor.

Wriedt Sørensen, L.
2009 Artemis in Cyprus in: T. Fischer-Hansen and B. Poulsen (eds.), From Artemis to Diana. The Goddess of Man and Beast, Copenhagen, 195-206.

Wright, G.R.H.
1992 Ancient Building in Cyprus, Leiden.

Yon, M.
1980 Zeus de Salamine in: R. Bloch (ed.), Recherches sur les religions de l'Antiquité classique, Genève-Paris, 85-103.
1992 The Goddess of the Salt-Lake in: G.C. Ioannides (ed.), Studies in Honour of V. Karageorghis, Nicosia, 301-6.
2009 Le culte impérial à Salamine, CCEC 39: 289-308.

Young, J. H. and Young, S. H.
1955 Terracotta Figurines from Kourion in Cyprus, Philadelphia.

INDEX OF ANCIENT AUTHORS

Actae Barnabae
20-21 – *The Twelve Patriarchs, Excerpts and Epistles, The Clementina, Apocrypha, Decretals, Memoirs of Edessa and Syriac Documents*, translated by P. Schaff, Ante-Nicene Fathers 8, Edinburgh, 1994.

Acts of the Apostles
13.5 – *ESV Study Bible*, Wheaton, 2008.

Antoninus Liberalis
Arkeophon: 39.1-6 – P. W. Wallance and A. G. Orphanides (eds.), *Sources for the History of Cyprus: Greek and Latin Texts to the Third Century A.D.*, Nicosia, 1990, 233-34.

Ammianus Marcellinus
14.8.14 – Ammianus Marcellinus, *History, Volume I: Books 14-19*, translated by J. C. Rolfe, Loeb Classical Library 300, Cambridge, 1950.

Appian
Bellum Civile: 5.1.9, 5.6.52 – Appian, *Roman History, Volume IV: The Civil Wars, Books 3.27-5*, translated by H. White, Loeb Classical Library 5, Cambridge, 1913.

REFERENCES

Arnobius
Adversus nationes: 5.19.2 – Arnobius of Sicca, *The Seven Books of Arnobius Adversus Gentes*, translated by A. Roberts and J. Donaldson, Ante-Nicene Christian library XIX, Edinburgh, 1871.

Cassius Dio
42.35.4-6 – Dio Cassius, *Roman History, Volume IV: Books 41-45*, translated by E. Cary and H.B. Foster, Loeb Classical Library 66, Cambridge, 1916.
49.32.4-5, 49.41.1-3 – Dio Cassius, *Roman History, Volume V: Books 46-50*, translated by E. Cary and H.B. Foster, Loeb Classical Library 82, Cambridge, 1917.
68.32.1-3 – Dio Cassius, *Roman History, Volume VIII: Books 61-70*, translated by E. Cary and H.B. Foster, Loeb Classical Library 176, Cambridge, 1925.

Catullus
68a.: 51-52 – *Catullus. Tibullus. Pervigilium Veneris*, translated by F.W. Cornish, J.P. Postgate, and J.W. Mackail, revised by G.P. Goold, Loeb Classical Library 6, Cambridge, 1913.

Chariton
Callirhoe: 8.2.7-9 – Chariton, *Callirhoe*, edited and translated by G.P. Goold, Loeb Classical Library 481, Cambridge, 1995.

Claudius Ptolemy
Geographia: 5.14.1-7 – P.W. Wallance and A.G. Orphanides (eds.), *Sources for the History of Cyprus: Greek and Latin Texts to the Third Century A.D.*, Nicosia, 1990, 230-31.

Clement of Alexandria,
Protrepticus: 2.29, 2.12-13, 3.40 – Clement of Alexandria, *The Exhortation to the Greeks. The Rich Man's Salvation. To the Newly Baptized*, translated by G.W. Butterworth, Loeb Classical Library 92, Cambridge, 1919.

Diogenianus
Corpus Paroemiographorum Graecorum I: 178 – P.W. Wallance and A.G. Orphanides (eds.), *Sources for the History of Cyprus: Greek and Latin Texts to the Third Century A.D.*, Nicosia, 1990, 229.

Eusebius
Historiae Ecclesiastica: 4.2 – Eusebius, *Ecclesiastical History, Volume I: Books 1-5*, translated by K. Lake, Loeb Classical Library 153, 1926.

Firmicus Maternus
De errore profanorum religionum: 10 – Julius Firmicus Maternus, *De errore profanarum religionum*, introduction, translation and commentary by R.E. Oster, Jr., Ma Thesis, Rice University, 1971.

Georgius Cyprius
Descriptio Orbis Romani: 1096-1110 – Georgii Cyprii, *Descriptio orbis Romani. Accedit Leonis Imperatoris Diatyposis genuina adhuc inedita*, commentario instruxit Henricus Gelzer, Lipsiae, 1890.

Hesiod
Theogony: 190-200 – Hesiod, *Theogony. Works and Days. Testimonia*, edited and translated by G.W. Most, Loeb Classical Library 57, Cambridge 2018.

Herodotus
Historiae: 5.113.1 – P.W. Wallance and A.G. Orphanides (eds.), *Sources for the History of Cyprus: Greek and Latin Texts to the Third Century A.D.*, Nicosia, 1990, 13.

Hesychius
Alexandrini lexicon: Karposis, Afroditos, omphalos, Malika–Hesychii, *Alexandrini Lexicon, Ed. minorem* curavit Mauricius Schmidt, Moritz, 1823-1888.

Hipponax
125-126 – *Archilochus, Semonides, Hipponax. Greek Iambic Poetry: From the Seventh to the Fifth Centuries BC*, edited and translated by D.E. Gerber, Loeb Classical Library 259, Cambridge, 1999.

Homeric Hymns
Homeric Hymn 5 To Aphrodite – *Homeric Hymns. Homeric Apocrypha. Lives of Homer*, edited and translated by M.L. West, Loeb Classical Library 496, Cambridge, 2003.

Horacy
Carm 1.7.21-29 – P.W. Wallance and A.G. Orphanides (eds.), *Sources for the History of Cyprus: Greek and Latin Texts to the Third Century A.D.*, Nicosia, 1990, 112.

Isocrates,
Evagoras: 18.50 – Isocrates, *Evagoras. Helen. Busiris. Plataicus. Concerning the Team of Horses. Trapeziticus. Against Callimachus. Aegineticus. Against Lochites. Against Euthynus. Letters*, translated by L.R. van Hook, Loeb Classical Library 373, Cambridge, 1945.

Josephus Flavius
Antiquitates Iudaicae: 13.284 – Josephus, *Jewish Antiquities, Volume V: Books 12-13*, translated by R. Marcus, Loeb Classical Library 365, Cambridge, 1943.

Lucian
De dea Syria 6 – Lucian, *Complete Works including The Syrian Goddesss* translated by H.A. Strong and J. Garstang, Delphi Classics, 2016.

Lycophron
450-494, 586-91 – *Callimachus (Hymns and Epigrams). Lycophron. Aratus*, translated by A.W. Mair and G.R. Mair, Loeb Classical Library 129, Cambridge, 1921.

Macrobius
Saturnalia, 1. 21 – Macrobius, *Saturnalia, Volume I: Books 1-2*, edited and translated by R.A. Kaster, Loeb Classical Library 510, Cambridge, 2011.

REFERENCES

Pausanias
Hellados Periegesis 8.5.2-3; 8.15.5-7 – P.W. Wallance and A.G. Orphanides (eds.), *Sources for the History of Cyprus: Greek and Latin Texts to the Third Century A.D.*, Nicosia, 1990, 199.
Hellados Periegesis 9. 41. 2-3 – P.W. Wallance and A.G. Orphanides (eds.), *Sources for the History of Cyprus: Greek and Latin Texts to the Third Century A.D.*, Nicosia, 1990, 200.

Photius Constantinopolitanus
190. 152b – Photius, *Bibliothèque, Tome III (Codices 186-222)*, edited and translated by R. Henry, Collection Byzantine, Paris, 1962.

Pliny Elder
Historia Naturalis 5.130 – P.W. Wallance and A.G. Orphanides (eds.), *Sources for the History of Cyprus: Greek and Latin Texts to the Third Century A.D.*, Nicosia, 1990, 140-41.

Plutarch,
Anthony – Plutarch, *Lives, Volume IX: Demetrius and Antony. Pyrrhus and Gaius Marius*, translated by B. Perrin, Loeb Classical Library 101, Cambridge, 1920.
Cato Minor 34-38 – Plutarch, *Lives, Volume VIII: Sertorius and Eumenes. Phocion and Cato the Younger*, translated by B. Perrin, Loeb Classical Library 100, Cambridge, 1919.
Life of Theseus 20.2-4 – Plutarch, *Lives, Volume I: Theseus and Romulus. Lycurgus and Numa. Solon and Publicola*, translated by B. Perrin, Loeb Classical Library 46, Cambridge, 1914.
Moralia 5.351-384 – Plutarch, *Moralia, Volume V: Isis and Osiris. The E at Delphi. The Oracles at Delphi No Longer Given in Verse. The Obsolescence of Oracles*, translated by F.C. Babbitt, Loeb Classical Library 306, Cambridge, 1936.

Porphyrios
De Abstinentia: 2.54 – Porphyry, *On abstinence from animal food*, translated by T. Taylor, London, 1965.

Stephanus of Byzantium
Ethnica: 380.4-6 – Stephani Byzantii, *Ethnica. Volumen III*, recensuit, Germanice vertit, adnotationibus indicibusque instruxit M. Billerbeck, Berlin, 2014.

Strabo
Geographica: 14.6.1-3, 14.6.5 – Strabo, *Geography, Volume VI: Books 13-14*, translated by H.L. Jones, Loeb Classical Library 223, Cambridge, 1929.

Swetonius
De vita Caesarum Titus –Suetonius, *Lives of the Caesars, Volume II: Claudius. Nero. Galba, Otho, and Vitellius. Vespasian. Titus, Domitian. Lives of Illustrious Men: Grammarians and Rhetoricians. Poets (Terence. Virgil. Horace. Tibullus. Persius. Lucan). Lives of Pliny the Elder and Passienus Crispus*, translated by J.C. Rolfe, Loeb Classical Library 38, Cambridge, 1914.

Tacitus
Annales 3.62 – Tacitus, *Histories: Books 4-5. Annals: Books 1-3*, translated by C.H. Moore and

J. Jackson, Loeb Classical Library 249, Cambridge, 1931.
Histories 2. 2-3 – Tacitus, *Histories: Books 1-3*, translated by C.H. Moore, Loeb Classical Library 111, Cambridge, 1925.

Talmud
Keritot 6a – *The William Davidson digital edition of the Koren Noé Talmud*, with commentary by Rabbi Adin Even-Israel Steinsaltz, www.sefaria.org.il.

Virgilius
Aeneida 1. 415-417 – Virgil, *Eclogues. Georgics. Aeneid: Books 1-6.*, translated by H.R Fairclough. Revised by G.P. Goold, Loeb Classical Library 63, Cambridge, 1916.

LIST OF ABBREVIATIONS

AJA	American Journal of Archaeology
BAR IS	British Archaeological Reports International Series
BCH	Bulletin de Correspondance Hellénique
BSA	Annual of the British School at Athens
CCEC	Cahiers du Centre d'Études Chypriotes
JHS	Journal of Hellenic Studies
JRS	Journal of Roman Studies
OpArch	Opuscula Archaeologica
RDAC	Reports of the Department of Antiquities, Cyprus
SIMA	Studies in Mediterranean Archaeology
ZPE	Zeitschrift für Papyrologie und Epigraphik

APPENDIX

The life-span of Cypriot sanctuaries from the Cypro-Archaic to the Roman period.

No on map	Site	Cypro-Archaic period	Cypro-Classical period	Hellenistic period	Roman period
1	Achna (south)	✓	✓	✓	✓
2	Amargetti—Petros Anthropos	✓	✓	✓	✓
3	Amathous-Acropolis	✓	✓	✓	✓
4	Amathous-Agora			✓	
5	Amathous-Agora			✓	✓
6	Amathous-gate				✓
7	Arsos	✓	✓	✓	✓
8	Chandria				✓
9	Chytroi-Skali	✓	✓	✓	✓
10	Golgoi-Hagios Photios	✓	✓	✓	✓
11	Idalion-Moutti tou Arvili	✓	✓	✓	✓
12	Idalion—City sanctuary	✓	✓	✓	✓
13	Keryneia-Regatikon	✓	✓	✓	✓
14	Kition	✓	✓	✓	✓
15	Kourion—Apollo Hylates	✓	✓	✓	✓
16	Larnaca-Salines	✓			
17	Ledra			✓	
18	Lefkoniko	✓	✓	✓	✓

cont. Appendix

No on map	Site	Cypro-Archaic period	Cypro-Classical period	Hellenistic period	Roman period
19	Lourodjina			×	×
20	Malloura	×	×	×	×
21	Nea Paphos Phabrica			×	×
22	Nea Paphos—Phanari			×	×
23	Nea Paphos—podium temple				×
24	Nea Paphos—Toumballos	×	×	×	×
25	Palaipaphos	×	×	×	×
26	Phasoula—Zeus Labranios				×
27	Pyla—Stavros	×	×	×	×
28	Pyroi-Elia—Marko	×	×	×	×
29	Rantidi—Lingrin tou Digeni	×	×	×	×
30	Rizokarpasso (Chelones)	×	×	×	×
31	Salamis—Zeus Temple	×	×	×	×
32	Soloi—Acropolis		×	×	×
33	Soloi—Cholades			×	×
34	Tamassos	×	×	×	×
35	Tamassos	×	×	×	×
36	Voni	×	×	×	×

PLATES

Plate 1. a) Palaipaphos Sanctuary II. Photo by the author; b) Palaipaphos—South stoa. Photo by the author.

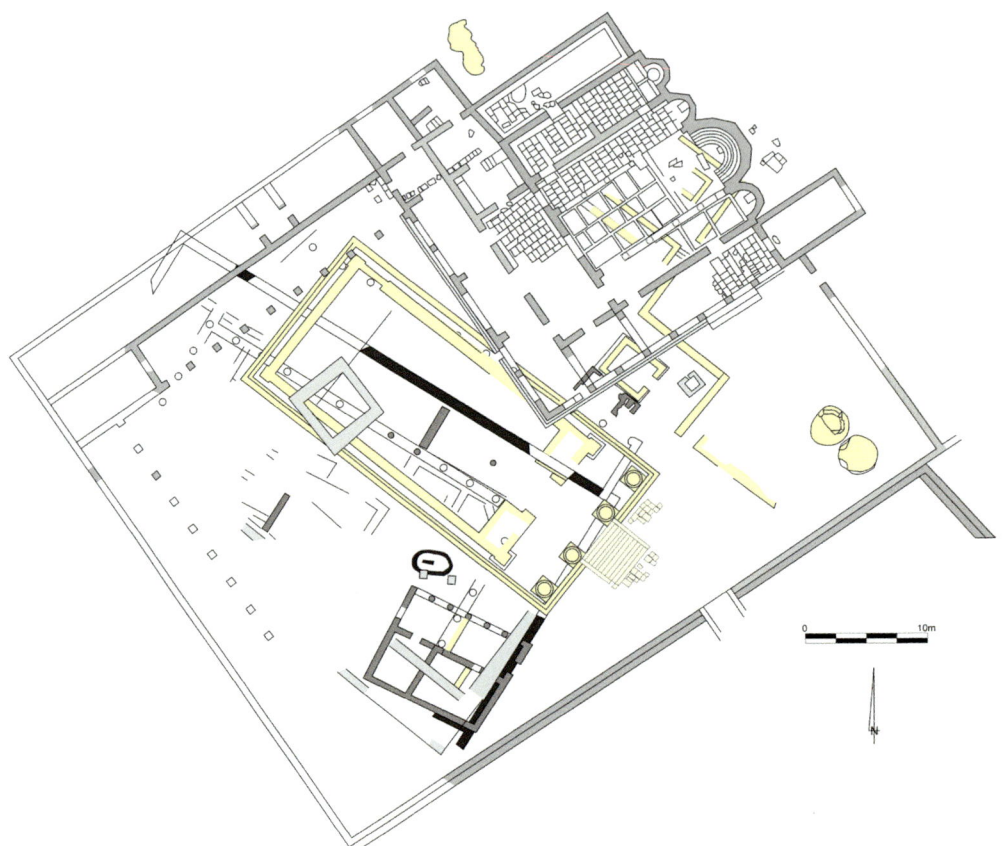

Plate 2. Amathous Acropolis – structures important during roman phase (in yellow).
Plan based on Aupert 2000, 60.

Plate 3. a) Petra Nabatean capital. Photo by the author;
b) Amathous acropolis. A reconstruction of a monumental stone vase. Photo by Anastasia Yukovleva.

Plate 4. Temple of Apollo Hylates—reconstruction. Photo by the author.

Plate 5. Petra tou Ramnou—the mythical birthplace of Aphrodite. Photo by the author.

Plate 6. a) Palaipaphos. Photo by the author; b) A baetyl from Sanctuary II. Museum in Kokulia. Photo by the author; c) Votary model of the temple from Palaipaphos. Museum in Koukulia. Photo by the author.

Plate 7. Panorama of the acropolis of Amathous. Photo by the author.

Plate 8. a) Remains of an altar in Sanctuary of Apollo Hylates at Kourion. Photo by the author;
b) Remains of Round Building—a placed where sacred trees possibly were planted. Photo by the author.

Plate 9. a) Salt Lake near Larnaca. Photo by the author; b) Kition—Kathari. Photo by the author.

Plate 10. A bronze statue of Septimius Sever from Chytroi. Cyprus Museum in Nicosia. Photo by the author.

Plate 11. The theatre of Salamis. Photo by the author.

Plate 12. a) Idalion—Ambelleri hill. Photo by the author;
b) A mosaic of representation of Theseus. Villa of Theseus. Nea Paphos. Photo by the author.